Gerhard Durlacher was born in Baden-Baden, Germany, in 1928. As a child he fled with his family to Holland, from where he was taken to a concentration camp. After the war he returned to Holland, where he taught sociology at the University of Amsterdam for many years. With *Stripes in the Sky*, Gerhard Durlacher begins his continuing reflection on the genocide of which he was a reluctant witness.

D1057357

STRIPES IN THE SKY

GERHARD DURLACHER

Translated by Susan Massotty

SERPENT'S
TAIL

British Library Cataloguing in Publication Data
Durlacher, Gerhard, *1928*–
Stripes in the sky.
1. Jews. Genocide, *1933–45* — Bibliographies
I. Title
940.531503924
ISBN 1-85242-202-5

First published 1985 by Meulenhoff Nederland bv, Amsterdam.

Copyright © 1985 by G.L. Durlacher and Meulenhoff Nederland bv

Translation copyright © 1991 by Susan Massotty

This edition first published 1991 by
Serpent's Tail, 4 Blackstock Mews, London N4

Set in 10/14pt Garamond by AKM Associates (UK) Ltd, London
Printed on acid-free paper by
Nørhaven A/S, Viborg, Denmark

CONTENTS

Eli, Eli, Lama sabachthani
My God, my God, why hast thou forsaken me!

STRIPES IN THE SKY

PROLOGUE

Underexposed images arise from my memory, alternated by glaring, overexposed scenes etched on my retina. Occasionally, my attempts to recognize and put these film clips in order are successful, albeit imperfect. The feelings I had then, the agony and fear, the helplessness and rage, the pain and misery, are buried deeply, like lava in a supposedly extinct volcano.

These images, accompanied by searing emotions, are triggered by the stories of my former fellow prisoners, by books, a photograph, an association.

Two books which set off these images in me were published in the fall of 1981: *The Terrible Secret* by Walter Laqueur and *Auschwitz and the Allies* by Martin Gilbert. The subtitles rule out any misunderstanding about the contents: *An Investigation into the Suppression of Information About Hitler's "Final Solution"* and *How the Allies Responded to the News of Hitler's Final Solution*, respectively. Two factual and sobering books about the murder of six million Jews between 1939 and 1945, what the world knew of the slaughter and how it reacted to the news.

I see us standing there in rows of five, pale from exhaustion, our ankles swollen, our heads spinning, our stomachs empty. We stood there for roll call together with the Russian prisoners. August 1944: the late afternoon sun reflected off their shaved heads. We count off: one time, two times, ten times. We are counted. Emil, the Polish *Blockälteste*,[1] beats the line into shape and, nervous, his voice hoarse, counts us as well. The *Blockführer*[2] counts us, beating the first and last person in every row on the head with his walking stick. We don't dare change places. Our thirst overpowers our hunger. We can forget the soup. Something is going on, because the sirens had sounded. We see through the stinking veil of smoke from Crematorium III that the sky is blue, and we grow unsteady or faint. Supporting our comrades takes up our last ounce of strength. Emil directs the sick to the last row and an SS man snarls at him. In the distance, we hear a rumble that sounds like thunder. We exchange knowing glances: Russian artillery in the Beskid mountains? They have to be close; after all, hadn't the reports from the airplane demolition squad been optimistic?

The hoarse barking of the Kapos and SS men is drowned out by the rhythmical hum in the sky, and suddenly we all see the white strands of sheep's wool that are drawn by almost invisible metal dots across the light blue sky. Hundreds of pairs of eyes follow these stripes until the SS men, screams pouring forth from their square jaws and raining down blows, start the counting off again.

Above us roars the mock thunder that gives our hearts the strength to keep on standing and brings an imperceptible grin to our faces. The roll call ends in the night, after the sirens have finished wailing again.

Three of the five prisoners who escaped are captured alive: Piechowiak, Wagschal and Kenner. Bloody and mutilated, they're brought back to our camp, Men's Camp Birkenau B II D.

On the evening of 8 August as we, dirty and exhausted and supporting or carrying our wounded, are being chased in rows of five under the *Arbeit macht frei* (Work sets you free) sign, we see two of them hanged. Singing, our hearts full of death, and accompanied by the camp orchestra, we march with non-seeing eyes past the two gallows. Their death is probably easier than that of Piechowiak in the hard-labor gang.

That same evening, the stripes again appear in the sky. Had they forgotten us, those on the outside and those above us? Were the oil refineries of Blechhammer and Trzebinia more important than we and our furnaces were? In the month that followed, they no longer burned night and day. The Jews of Hungary had almost left their earthly suffering behind them. The last transport from Westerbork arrived: 1,019 people, 470 of whom did not immediately fall prey to the flames. One of these was Anne Frank, at that time one of the unknowns in the ocean of death.

I hardly knew what was happening at the time. My perception was clouded, my emotions numbed. I recorded the terrible events without letting them into my head and heart.

Now, after almost forty years, an occasional page from the archives falls from the mouldering safe of my memory.

My companions and I in the cart squad heard the

bombardment of Monowitz that Gilbert describes in his book. On 13 September 1944 we dared to hope that liberation might be near. For a short time, we felt behind the glassy façade of our brains that there was still an "outside" and that Auschwitz was not on another planet.

Panting and driven by curses and blows, we'd spent the entire morning transporting wood and tar paper. I no longer know where we were loading the material, but it couldn't have been far from the railroad siding known as the "Ramp", the transfer point to eternity. The SS man disappeared, probably in order to take cover, and we stood there as if we were awaiting a warm summer rain.

The bombardment of IG Farben couldn't have lasted very long. All around us was wind, dust and noise. We had felt no fear.

This is how farmers must feel when rain suddenly falls after their prayers. The few bombs that landed on Birkenau led us to believe that the crematoria had been hit, but this dream sequence was quickly shattered. All that remained to us was disillusionment, dust-filled eyes and a fragment of a shell or a bomb as big as your hand that Jiri D. had picked up. "Go, for God's sake, but get going!" shrieked the Kapo in Yiddish, and the overloaded cart with us as sled dogs slowly began to move.

The question of whether those on the outside and those above had forgotten us has long been on the tip of many a tongue. Why it was actually posed only a few years ago and has still been only partially answered now is a matter of conjecture.

The most obvious reason for this painful postponement can

probably be attributed to the laws regulating historical archives in the countries concerned. The English archives and certain American archives have only recently released some of the documents from the skeleton of their modern history.

By reason of their past and present work, both historians, Laqueur and Gilbert, are eminently suited to carry out the research work. The former is Director of the Institute of Contemporary History, alias the Wiener Library, in London (the institute which was one of the foremost sources of information on Nazi Germany during the Second World War). The latter, as the official biographer of Winston Churchill, had access to secret documents which a layman would not even have dared dream were preserved for posterity.

Another reason the terrible secret was kept so long reminds me of what happened when the Sphinx asked Oedipus a question: his correct answer caused her to tumble from her pedestal. The riddle had been solved, but he paid a bitter price for his enlightenment, and he was left without any illusions.

We too now know the answer to our question and we also have a bitter price to pay. We have lost the few illusions remaining to us.

Laqueur and Gilbert were tormented by the same questions, but the subtitles to their books suggest that Gilbert (born in 1936) is more resilient than his fifteen-year-older colleague Laqueur. To a certain extent, the subtitle of Laqueur's book, *An Investigation into the Suppression of Information About Hitler's "Final Solution"*, is also his own suppression. His story ends in December 1942, a time frame that he defends by arguing that "the majority of Jews in Eastern Europe knew [about the mass slaughter], so did millions of Germans and other residents of Nazi-occupied Europe." Moreover, he meticulously avoids the question of what these people did with this horrible knowledge.

I can certainly understand that Laqueur, born in the Weimar Republic in 1921, his youth crushed by the Nazis whose clutches he barely managed to escape, might need this rationalization and suppression. Nevertheless, the December 1942 date is difficult to accept. Neither I nor any of my fellow inmates knew about the purgatory of Birkenau before we passed through the main gate. It was only when the prisoners Vrba, Wetzler, Rosin and Mordowicz made a successful escape in April 1944 and their reports were brought to the attention of the Allies that no one in government or military circles or from among the reading or listening public could still claim in all good conscience: "We didn't know anything."

Martin Gilbert gave his book the subtitle: *How the Allies Responded to the News of Hitler's Final Solution.* Gilbert cites one of these "responses," made on 7 September 1944 by A.R. Dew, an English diplomat later killed in an accident while en route to the Yalta conference: "In my opinion a disproportional amount of time of the Office is wasted on dealing with these wailing Jews" (Foreign Office Papers 371/42817, WR 993). No wonder we felt abandoned.

At first glance, Gilbert's and Laqueur's books appear to overlap somewhat, but because of the questions they pose, their investigations supplement each other.

"In this book," Laqueur writes, "I have tried to provide answers to the following questions:

— When did the information about the 'Final Solution' first
become known to Jews and non-Jews?

— Through what channels was it transmitted?

— What was the reaction of those who received the news?"

He also sets himself the task of showing that, despite the
secrecy and disinformation, a large part of Nazi Germany's
population could have known and already did know early in
the war that mass murders were being carried out. According
to Laqueur, the question arises of what the meaning of
"knowing" and "believing" is, or in other words, how much
credibility was accorded the gruesome message in Germany
and the rest of the world.

The rest of the world, in particular, could have done so
much and did so little to help increase European Jewry's
chance of survival.

When reading Laqueur's book, I could not help but feel that
his own need to suppress the most terrible part of the secret,
the mass extermination, induced him to apply a more
charitable analysis than I and many others consider justified.

According to SS data, 2,500,000 Jews had been deported and
had perished before the end of 1942. The majority of the
victims had been dragged out of Poland, Russia and the Baltic
countries and had been executed by *Einsatzgruppen*.[3]

The chimneys of the death camps Chelmno, Belzec,
Majdanek, Sobibor and Treblinka smoked continuously. More
than 200,000 Jews from Germany and the occupied territories
were deported, and more than 2,000,000 Polish and Russian
Jews were wiped off the face of the earth.

Despite Nazi codewords, censored radio broadcasts,
newspapers and postal communications and despite the

interception of couriers and telegrams, countless persons knew about the atrocities in the East. Thousands of people passed on messages through dozens of channels, including by word of mouth. Through the stories and letters of husbands, sons and brothers, the families of those in the Wehrmacht and SS were often better informed than they would ever have dared admit after the war.

But clergymen, members of the underground, couriers, smugglers and railway workers also passed first- or second-hand messages through to the West or carried the bad news to the Polish ghettos still in existence. By using material in English, American, German and Israeli archives and talking with numerous people involved, Laqueur was able to reconstruct a network of information channels that convinces us that at the end of 1942, a large part of the process involved in the Final Solution could already have been known.

But were the facts actually known, or rather were the facts believed in Allied political circles? Laqueur gives an indication of the psychological resistance that could be seen even in such a fair-minded man as Judge Frankfurter, a leading American lawyer and Supreme Court judge. Jan Karski, a Polish officer and courier, who brought him the news of the mass murders in Europe, was told that Frankfurter *could* not believe him.

Only a few people in the West grasped the magnitude of the tragedy before the end of 1942. They included Zygielbojm and Schwarzbart, two Jewish members of the Polish Parliament who had escaped to London where they expressed their well-founded fear that the massacres in 1942 were only the beginning of the catastrophe. They mobilized the English press and a small segment of public opinion.

Driven to despair by his feeling that the world was standing by passively as the Jews disappeared, Zygielbojm took his life in May 1943, after the SS had smothered the uprising in the Warsaw ghetto in blood and flames. His moving letter of farewell appeared in the press, but the reactions to the atrocities continued to be tepid.

The vast majority of the news of the disaster that came from the East wound up on the desks of Gerhard Riegner, a young German-Jewish lawyer from Berlin, and his thirty-year-older colleague, Richard Lichtheim, both of whom were representatives of the Jewish Agency in Geneva. The bad tidings reached them via informants, ranging from industrialists and journalists to couriers and smugglers, and they attempted to direct these toward heads of state and ministers, often with the help of intermediaries, such as Chief Rabbi Stephen Wise and Judge Frankfurter. Theirs must have been a frightfully heavy burden, for the eardrums and hearts of those in Whitehall and the White House were made of granite.

Of course, the message was hard to bear and thus hard to believe; but was this the only reason for the disbelief, the defensive reactions and the skepticism of Roosevelt and Eden and their officials and diplomats?

Laqueur is more charitable and more tolerant in his analysis than Gilbert or Wasserstein. That government circles and the media in England and the United States reacted with some reticence to the bloody news in the early years of the war is not incomprehensible. The argument that it was difficult to verify the information and that the intelligence service operated inadequately may carry some weight, although we still need to wait and see what the unopened parts of the Allied archives will reveal if they are ever released. But the related argument that the Allies did not wish to be reduced to repeating the error of propagandizing the atrocities of the First World War, when not only the gutter press but also such writers as Toynbee and Buchan wrote about the German barbarity during the attack on Belgium in August 1914, seems to me to be grossly exaggerated. Does this not put the naivety of the Allies in too innocent a light?

Leaving aside the fact that the German invasion of Belgium in 1914 was excessively brutal, the period described by Laqueur was "quite a different cup of blood".

Whitehall and Washington knew what the plans of the Nazis were: Hitler's *Mein Kampf* had been available for fifteen years and Rauschning's *Gespräche mit Hitler* [4] for ten years. The invasion of Czechoslovakia and Poland, *Kristallnacht* and the euthanasia program were still fresh in people's memories. The Third Reich's concentration camps were already notorious, and Eicke's Death Head Regiment and the *Einsatz-gruppen* already had more than two million deaths on their conscience.

There is little point in adding dozens of items to this list. It should have been sufficient to make reports of mass slaughters in Poland plausible to any reasonable, well-informed citizen without raking up associations with atrocity propaganda. And what about governments with highly trained diplomats and secret services? Was it naivety or feigned fear that the citizenry would confuse news coverage with such propaganda? Was it plain indifference to the fate of millions or should the explanation be viewed considerably more cynically—and realistically?

Laqueur's analysis is terrifying enough, but it leaves me feeling that he hesitates to draw the bottom line. On page 201, he writes: "Even after it had been accepted in London and Washington that the information about the mass slaughter was correct, the British and US governments showed much concern that it should not be given too much publicity." Why all the concern about publicity? For the Jews in these countries, with their fear of being branded as scaremongers, this is understandable. But what about the non-Jewish allies? It is precisely questions such as these that torment us now as much as they did then.

As far as I am concerned, Gilbert's book has answered many agonizing questions. The Sphinx has been cast down and all illusions have been shattered. The pages have stacked themselves like lead weights in my mind. How must Gilbert have felt when writing those three hundred and fifty pages? With terrifying precision, he chronologically reports the events, conversations, notes and memoranda of the Allies dealing with the Final Solution from May 1942 to May 1945.

Political cynicism, opportunism, slackness, indifference, hate and naivety were ranged against the despair and destruction of the persecuted and their relatives, friends and sympathizers.

The few morally upright civil servants and government officials were thwarted in their efforts to do more than think in strategic and political terms. In addition to describing these catastrophic reports, Gilbert demonstrates how step by step and from report to report, the names of the death camps were turned into flaming nightmares.

It is not until 1942 that the Allies are able to reach, with difficulty, an agreement on a joint declaration condemning Germany for its policy of extermination and threatening reprisal and punishment. Auschwitz is not yet mentioned in this statement. It is only a name on a map, albeit a map of strategic importance.

The declaration issued after so much effort does not stop the policy of extermination in any way. The endlessly long trains with their cattle cars keep on rolling to the gas chambers in Poland, whatever course the war takes.

It appears that escape from Bulgaria and Romania in 1942 and 1943 is not impossible. But the passage through Turkey and entry to what was then Palestine are blocked by barriers made of granite. Lord Moyne and Oliver Stanley, respectively Secretary of State for the Colonies and Secretary of State for War in the British war cabinet, do not even allow in the small quota of immigrants set down in the White Paper of 1939.

In spite of the intercession, political pressure and even pleas of Chaim Weizmann, Moshe Shertok and myriad others, the gate to life remained closed to all but a few hundred children, and even that needed the personal intervention of Winston Churchill. In the meantime, the rusty transport ships with hundreds of refugees on board either sank in the Black Sea or were turned back.

Turkey and Great Britain were implacable, Middle East politics appeared to be secure and Haj Amin el Husseini, the Great Mufti of Jerusalem, friend and confidant of Hitler, Himmler and Eichmann, had been appeased.

But all the gates in the West were also shut tight. The United States and Britain sealed off their coasts to Jewish refugees, and between 1933 and 1945, Switzerland accepted only a few celebrities and children, a total of five thousand souls.

The Vichy government in France did not watch passively, but systematically sent first the Jews without French passports and then those with French passports to death via Drancy. Several thousand fled over the border to the areas around Grenoble and Nice governed by the Italians. And the Italians turned a blind eye to this practice, or sometimes even offered active assistance. The absurdities of history!

In 1944, the best-kept secret in the Second World War slowly begins to leak out. In spite of reassuring postcards from Auschwitz, postmarked from nonexistent wooded places and dated (as we now know and are able to read) a week after the sender had left this life, the meaning of Auschwitz-Birkenau is clear to some Slovaks. Yet the reports from Slovakia and Hungary are still being considered in the West as feverish hallucinations.

The pieces of the puzzle only begin to fall into place in April 1944 when Rudolf Vrba and three of his companions are able to make their escape and put together a highly accurate report about the systematic murder in Birkenau. Checks and double-checks, interrogations and cross-interrogations precede the sending of the report. The fear on the part of the partisans and Jews of being met with disbelief in Switzerland, England and the United States is tragicomic.

It takes more than two months for the bad tidings to reach the Allied capitals, and in the meantime the crematoria and incineration pits swallow up ten to twenty thousand every day. Fast action is necessary. Hundreds of thousands of Jews in Hungary and thousands from other German-occupied territories could still be saved. Shertok and Weizmann, on behalf of the Jewish Agency, ask Eden to bomb the railway lines to Auschwitz as well as its crematoria and gas chambers.

John Pehle, Executive Director of the US War Refugee Board, serves as intermediary to John J. McCloy, Undersecretary of War (and in 1945 US High Commissioner in Germany, where he was the protector of A. Speer and his family and where he granted pardons to such war criminals as *Einsatzgruppen* commanders Jost and Blum after they had been sentenced to death), in order to get the Americans to use their bombers against these targets.

Similar pleas come from Switzerland, Poland and Hungary.

McCloy in Washington and Lord Sinclair in London react slowly and evasively with such arguments as:

— the situation has to be studied
— the bombing of railway junctions is not effective (because they are quickly repaired)
— the lines of communication are too long, which means the planes cannot be refueled
— the lines of communication are too long, which involves too many risks.

Bombing of the crematoria in Auschwitz is impossible because:

— the planes would have to fly too low on account of the antiaircraft guns
— too many prisoners would be killed

— the targets cannot be distinguished clearly through the
  smoke
— reconnaissance is not possible
— no planes are available, as they are needed to wage the
  war in the West
— there would not be enough volunteers to man these
  risky flights, and lastly
— the type of precision bombing required would not fall
  within the range of technical feasibility.

Gilbert, along with Lichtenstein, Wyman and American Air
Force officers who flew over Auschwitz in 1944, all disprove
these arguments with irrefutable evidence.

This is not the place to present these arguments at great
length. For those of us who in August 1944 saw those white
stripes of hope and heard the distant thunder of freedom, I
would like to put forward only two of the most poignant.

Gilbert discovered aerial photographs in the archives of the
Foreign Office and in the Air Force archives of the United
States and Great Britain which had been taken before and after
the bombing of the oil refineries and factories of Monowitz,
Blechhammer and Trzebinia.

The photos of Auschwitz-Birkenau, dated May through
September 1944, are highly accurate, showing the smoking
crematoria and the lines of people awaiting death. The quality
was excellent, for its time. Only no one seems to have noticed
those lines of people or the crematoria.

Who flew those bombers and where did they come from?
The answer is almost too simple, because it refutes the
arguments so easily. As early as 1943, the Americans had
prepared Operation Pointblank, aimed at undermining

Germany's oil position. The first series of reconnaissance photos taken in the region of Auschwitz in April 1944 clearly show the camp together with the adjacent industrial areas. After the invasion of Italy, the Allies had access to the airfield in Foggia, from which they could easily have flown via Poltava—behind the Russian lines—over the industrial areas around Auschwitz. It was this base that was used in the beginning of August 1944, during Operation Frantic, to provide assistance to the resistance troops in Warsaw.

The losses in men and material were relatively light. The bombing was a success.

The stray bombs that landed on Birkenau were merely a result of technical error; while attempting to evade the German antiaircraft guns, an allied pilot released his bomb load.

*   *   *

The feeling that the world more or less discreetly turns the other way or watches unmoved while hundreds of thousands of people are systematically being killed all around you and that you yourself know that every day you are still alive is a cruel trick of fate is something that cannot adequately be expressed in words.

Seething anger passes over into resignation and indifference, but if you leave the hell alive, you look back in bewilderment and incomprehension, either cynically or apathetically, but in any case impotently.

It is difficult to determine what attitude to take to the people you meet after such disasters. Whose side were they on then?

Did they watch or look the other way? Did they go along or did they resist?

The questions stick in your throat. Distrust and repression do not go away.

Distancing yourself, being objective, can help. It cools the wounds. This is the reason for this speculative epilogue without any scholarly pretensions.

Why did so many in the countries of the Axis powers, so many in the countries of the Allies and in the occupied territories remain silent?

For Germany in particular, the explanation seems simple: the fear of becoming a victim of the terror oneself as punishment for talking and knowing was justified. But in other countries and among the victims, Jews and Gypsies, this fear was unwarranted.

Laqueur and Gilbert clearly show that many more people, including "ordinary" people, knew about the Nazi atrocities than was supposed. Why all this silence?

Words such as "sadism," "cowardice," "indifference" and "opportunism" are not sufficient, although they cannot simply be discarded. A better explanation is that people whose emotions are still functioning cannot accept messages such as these without physical and mental damage.

A world in which the aged, the ill, children and pregnant women are destroyed as useless garbage, in which every human dignity is jeered at, in which a human being is nothing more than vermin-ridden cattle, no longer useful once it has consumed its own muscle tissue, can only be faced up to by a few.

Reports about what was happening "over there" cannot be accepted for they undermine all our values.

Even a new arrival in Auschwitz or the other extermination camps who had passed the selection for the gas chamber could not believe the first few days that the smoking chimneys did not belong to factories. He interpreted the stories snarled at him by other prisoners as some kind of gruesome initiation rite. When the grim reality dawned on him, night also fell over his spirit, just as it did mine. To a certain extent, this psycho-logical safety valve works as a means of self-preservation.

Another mechanism that promotes silence is the uncertainty about what others have seen or heard. Naturally, one person had more, or more reliable, information than another and he attached a certain degree of credibility to it, but that did not have to stop anyone from letting his voice be heard.

On the other hand, the uncertainty about what others do or do not know can reduce you to silence. It could thus create a situation in which people assumed without reason that their knowledge of the mass cruelties was not shared by others, or exactly the opposite, that everyone did share this knowledge.

It then takes courage and determination to open your mouth and protest.

The dilemma of who will believe me if I am the only one to think the incredible and who will save me from ridicule or punishment if I reveal what everyone knows could not be overcome without great moral strength.

It was precisely this strength that was a condition for passive and active resistance and—unfortunately—it was possessed by very few.

THE BEGINNING OF A JOURNEY

Westerbork, 3 October 1942, day of horror. Twelve thousand men, women and children, sitting, lying, draping themselves over battered suitcases and knapsacks. Grimy and sweaty. Tears run dry in the dust of unshaved cheeks. The call of first names, last names, place names. Quarrels over a few inches of space, a sip of water, a spoonful of food. People in endless lines or tight clusters in front of the soup kettles. Green, yellow and blue enamel bowls like Chinese lanterns in the hands of the waiting.

Thousands looking for wives and children, for barracks and dormitories, for water and food, for washrooms and latrines. Brown wooden barracks reeking of tar, crammed with wobbly iron scaffolds: three tiers of beds composed of angle irons, crossbars and weak springs. People wriggling between the bars, arguing heatedly about dividing two beds among six sleepers or sitting miserably on the edge because the overburdened structure has caved in. Stew in the food bowl. Without salt, onions or meat, but with peelings and sand. Thirst, dust and a shortage of water.

A steady stream of new arrivals who reduce the amount of

space. Stupid, because they don't yet know which barrack to go to, which faucet to use. Our two-hour head start makes us feel less insecure.

My parents on the lookout for acquaintances, to build false security out of collective ignorance. Searching for suitcases which were left next to the railroad track, miles away from the entrance to the camp, entrusted to men in overalls wearing caps and with armbands on their left arms.

Guarding the knapsacks, I'm in the grip of fantasies about being deserted in a forest of people. An aimless ice floe, adrift from the past and the future. How did I wind up here, in this godforsaken point in time and space?

My umbilical cord to time was cut twenty-four hours earlier. The shock and consternation weren't as great as I'd imagined in the preceding weeks and months. The arrest was different, calmer. Like a menacing but inevitable natural disaster.

It was fairly light outside. No later than about five in the afternoon, an hour at which you think: they won't come anymore today. But they did come: one of the *Grünen* [5] with two Dutch policemen. We'd heard them crunching over the gravel, so they only had to give a short ring. Somebody, my mother I think, was already at the door, because why should you let them kick in a perfectly good door?

One of the policemen, standing half in the entrance hall, asked: "Do Arthur Israël Durlacher, his wife Erna Sarah Durlacher née Solomonica, his son Gerhard Israël Durlacher, Mrs Ilse Sarah Maltenfort née Solomonica, Hans Israël Fleischmann and Herman Israël Feiner [6] live here?" An unnecessarily long question which struck me as threatening and ludicrous at the same time.

I can no longer recall exactly what happened next, but I understood that we had to be packed within a few hours and that one of the policeman would be present the whole time. To this day I still detest knapsacks and packing lists, just as I detest a number of items which have become all too familiar: uniforms, barbed wire, lookout towers.

The Jewish Council had already made the packing lists available months before. You had to make the knapsacks yourself. How could you get hold of canvas and who was willing to sew it together for you? Who wanted to trade your eiderdowns for wool blankets? Where could you still buy camping utensils and enamel bowls?

What kind of grim picnic was awaiting us?

After an indistinct exchange of words, the green-uniformed German and his Dutch helper disappeared. The policeman who stayed behind began to make clumsy excuses. He couldn't do anything about it, he'd been given his orders; we weren't to make trouble for him by trying to escape or get in touch with the neighbors; we weren't to use the telephone. In short, we should be glad that we had gotten such a humane policeman. And oh, how law-abiding we were. Imagine that he might have been scolded by his boss or by a German.

Later, Hans Fleischmann told us that he had hidden an army pistol, left over from his service days in the Austrian Army, in a packing crate, but that he hadn't considered using it to save himself. Knowing the kind of reprisals that would ensue, he hadn't wanted to endanger us.

Fleishmann had arrived, penniless and hungry, in the

Netherlands in 1939 at almost the same time as our other guest, housemate, companion in adversity, friend and "uncle", Herman Feiner. A few months earlier, in the aftermath of *Kristallnacht*, my aunt (my mother's sister) had moved in with us. My parents had managed to get her over the border by petitioning the Dutch Attorney General, Goseling, and having an audience with the Crown. Totally destitute, she came to us in Rotterdam and was able to move in to the room in which a few months earlier death had delivered my grandmother from her fear of the Gestapo, a fear that seemed absurd to me, a boy of ten.

Fleischmann and Feiner also slipped over the border with their suitcases and their ten Reichsmarks just in time. How they, accustomed as they were to a sumptuous standard of living, could live on the charity of the Jewish Council (or whatever its predecessor was called in 1939) remains a mystery to me.

Feiner could give a lively account of elegant dinners at Kempinski's restaurant and of his colleagues in Berlin, where until Hitler's arrival he had been a director and playwright and where he was on friendly terms with everything and everyone in the theater world. Now, his friends in the émigré cabaret in Scheveningen, Max Ehrlich, Kurt Liliën, Rudolf Nelson, Camilla Spira and Willy Rosen, led simple lives. They had managed to drag Feiner over the border, and I believe they also helped their colleague and friend from the Viennese *Volkstheater*, Hans Fleischmann, in his escape. Both men whiled away the time in their perfect hand-made suits as lodgers in Rotterdam.

My parents became acquainted with them during a musical

benefit for the refugees aboard the *St Louis*, who had drifted over the ocean for six months and were obliged to accept Holland, Belgium, France or England as their place of refuge instead of safe Cuba. Months before the German invasion, the two men were guests at our table, and by 10 May 1940 they were much more than friends; they had become family.

What were those bustling meals like on Friday evenings before the war? The table was pulled out to its maximum length, and ten or twelve people sat around it, conversing, gesturing, chewing, talking politics. Sometimes the roar of Hitler's or Goebbels' voice came out of the radio's loud-speaker, and everyone held their breath and hardly dared eat. After all, these were the weather forecasts on the looming fire storm, and each and every one was trying to guess whether it would subside or engulf us in its flames.

The guests from the Holland-America hotel—the cavernous, chilly building that offered the destitute refugees from the *St Louis* a leaky roof and drafty rooms—were especially gloomy. Their failed attempt to flee over the ocean had become a nightmare. They felt the wolves even closer by than we did.

Their banishment to the camp of Westerbork, less than thirty miles from the German border, under the pressure of the Dutch government and the approving eyes of the Jewish Council, must have given them the feeling of having been abandoned by God and the world. That feeling, which physically manifests itself as if too little blood is flowing through your veins and which makes your heart pump wildly, is fear. On 10 May 1940 I learned to recognize it in all its intensity, more so than in my childhood in Germany when

."Hitler youths" hounded me, jeered at me and hit me like the unprotected quarry I was.

To me, the beginning of the war is a blue sky with gray cotton dots, with the dull thud of antiaircraft guns and the panting voice of the radio commentator as background noise to the overexcited voices of my parents and aunt. The only one who could summon up some calm was Fleischmann, who had spent the night of 8–9 May with us with a premonition of doom. He was the only one who knew what war meant, though we were soon to learn.

On the other side of the River Schie, on the construction site where only one or two days earlier I had waded through the mud with friends, there was a machine-gun nest with three very young soldiers, still neat and trim in their uniforms. A few days later, I saw them again. Bloody, lying next to each other, sullied by death. A hundred yards further away, next to the Italian ice-cream store where I had squandered my pocket money the previous summer, was a garage. My father's dark-green Chevrolet was parked there awaiting our flight.

At first, the hostilities were paralyzing. Feiner, his voice hardened by fear, had joined us and urged us to flee. Discussions and quarrels over chances and risks, tears and migraines and in the background enervating news or enervating silences. The loudspeaker announced a curfew. The street was out of bounds to German Jews as well as to their enemies, the German citizens who were already living here in those first days of May. A crude and heartless prohibition. After all, our passports had already been branded with a huge "J" a year before that.

Benumbed like rabbits caught in a strong beam of light, we waited and waited. Escape appeared to be fraught with danger. Childish expectations about the impregnability of Holland's "Water Line"[7] were uttered as gospel truth. The days were covered in a veil of fear. At about one o'clock in the afternoon of 14 May the veil was rent by the sharp crack of antiaircraft guns and the sound of heavy thunder. We ran downstairs to the protective embrace of the recessed brick doorway. Crushed in either corner, avoiding the stairwell, we waited for the big boom, while the antiaircraft guns got louder and louder. My imagination didn't stretch far enough to encompass my mutilation by fire or high-explosive bombs, let alone death. The only thing that flashed through my mind was: let it come, let it be over.

Then, a few awful tremors, rubble, plaster, stones and dust; especially dust and silence. In the distance, sounds of thunder, voices screaming. An elderly neighbor lying motionless on the ground. Cracks in the walls through which you could see inside. Glass everywhere, and not a stick of furniture in place. The telephone is dangling from a painting. My dog has disappeared. Then suddenly a loud command from Fleischmann: "Duck! In the corner!" He spreads himself over us. Pounding airplane engines and a shrieking whistle. Once again there are tremors and thundering noises, but further away than the first time. The house sways like a ship in a storm but remains standing. More dust and rubble and then it's over. Except for a sound like an atonal choir in the distance. Shaken, pale and dusty, we look at each other, at ourselves, at the house ripped wide open. Nobody in the building is seriously wounded. The old lady gets a pill from her daughter and comes to life again. The bombardment of Rotterdam is over.

Everyone goes outside. Man-sized craters in front of the house. My dog is missing. Are there wounded further away? What's happened? Groups of people on the street talking to each other. The word "capitulation" is uttered. What does it mean?

A friend of my parents, who lived a few streets away, came to offer help. He, Dutch and not Jewish and to us all-knowing, advised us to try to get away via Ijmuiden.

Virtually without any luggage, my father holding on tightly to the leather vanity case—mysteriously called "Ezekiel"— which was stuffed with papers and valuables, we walked almost stealthily, keeping to the houses, to the garage on the other side of the Schie. We were driven by a fear of bomb craters and falling stones, but mainly by a fear of being stopped. Were you allowed to be outside, even if your house was in ruins? These five-hundred yards were eerie. I was dry-mouthed, choked with fear.

Tension and shock prevented my father from driving the car out of the garage with his customary verve, but once we got going, his nervousness gave way to an icy calm, which was also transmitted to us. Not a word was said about everything that had been left behind. It was forgotten in a moment, even though every piece of furniture had been cherished, even to excess, since my earliest childhood.

We drove through Blijdorp in the direction of Schiebroek. In the distance the drawbridge, open like a rat trap. Groups of soldiers. Halt. Ice-cold fear runs up and down our spines. A noncommissioned officer, not unfriendly, sticks his head through the window and seems to understand the situation.

My mother does the talking. Her heavy accent and drawn face make identification and explanation unnecessary. He was sorry, but he couldn't help us: the bridge had been destroyed, traffic was impossible; perhaps the Bergweg or the bridge over the Meuse?

Back, but not past our house. Fear of being recognized. Via the Walenburgerweg to the Bergweg. People running, shots; probably a fight with German parachutists. People gesture to us: "Go away, danger." A loud bang, a grazing shot along the beautifully polished mudguard. Which I thought a shame.

Ijmuiden appeared to be impossible to reach. Where else could we go? Zeeland? My father knew the road to the Meuse bridge. Hadn't we spent countless Sunday afternoons on that island with close relatives, my mother accompanying my father and his cousin on the piano as they practiced Verdi duets or Lehar operettas?

I don't know how close we got to the Meuse bridge, but it stayed out of reach. Cars, bicycles and pedestrians, everyone was turned back. In the distance marines, their rifles at the ready. Explosions and smoke. Fear and doubt among all those in our car. My father, as hoarse as someone with stage fright before a song recital and as white as a sheet, turned the car around and tried to find a way to the Van Weelstraat, where my uncle lived.

As in a feverish dream, I see flashes of Rotterdam burning. The neighborhood where the family lives hasn't been hit. They have even reinforced the cellar in their house. Such foresight surprised us. Space is limited, but there's no other sanctuary. My father attempts to tell what's happened, bursts into tears and suddenly faints. The beginning of the end was upon us.

Now, more than forty years after this devastating episode, the spring of 1940 appears to be a blurred series of slides. I see my parents looking for another place to live, a flat or a ground-level apartment in Blijdorp: the joy of the new; and the disappointing failures—already rented or unaffordable. The empty rooms that would have to be filled with overly heavy furniture dating from grandfather's time. The furnished suite on the Heemraadsingel with six beds spread throughout the rooms and a bathroom that was difficult to reach. Every time there was an air raid, I had to be helped, dizzy and with my insides churning, to the bathroom. Our return home to the patched up and battered house on the Schieweg, with its cemented cracks and the smell of fresh putty and unseasoned boards.

The evening of our return, an old classmate of my mother's, a pianist and conductor, fills the house with Smetana and Schubert *lieder*. Fortunately for him, he can't spend the night and drives out of our lives in his antiquated dark-green Fiat. With us waving from the sidewalk.

The same evening, a fierce storm blows up over the city. I lie fearfully in my bed, awakened by the thunder and with a premonition of disaster. Was that the throbbing sound of bombers? Or was it my imagination? When you're eleven years old, you're no longer supposed to wake up your parents because you're afraid of thunder or imagined noises. My parents grumble: it's two o'clock in the morning, it's only your imagination, nonsense. I can't be persuaded and lie somewhat later between them, comforted by the hardness of the wooden sides of the beds. I remain uneasy; I still hear the inaudible. A booming clap of what sounds like thunder flings us out of the beds. Flying glass and rubble, a tremor, rain and wind in the bedroom. The beds have collapsed. We run down the back staircase. The hard bouclé carpet is full of grit and splinters. My foot is bleeding. Down below, it looks as if time has stood still since 14 May, only this time it was stray English bombs. I can't remember the hours after that. In the morning, I have a bandaged foot and my parents are still in their nightclothes.

The weeks that follow are underexposed. Once again, the same suite on the Heemraadsingel, once again the dizziness and once again the airplane noise and the sirens playing havoc with my bowels. Fleischmann bent over my school atlas. Where is it still safe in Holland? Where are there woods you can hide in, where are there enough people so that you aren't conspicuous? July goes by like a cloud of dust; did I really have my birthday and did the time after that really exist?

Then: a large white painted house on the Loolaan in Apeldoorn, a suite of rooms "with use of kitchen". The landlady is more bad-tempered than good-tempered; not rude as long as she smells money, but as soon as she fears that the flow is drying up, her voice changes. Her short-sighted fish-like eyes and her abundant gums strike more fear into my mother than the torrent of words she only half under-stands. Our neighbor, an elderly, friendly widow who looks like a peasant and has veined cheeks and round eyes, comes to tea. She and our landlady look daggers at each other. Then many things change surprisingly quickly. The neighbor's daughter, a large girl in her twenties whose continual blush is either natural or due to shyness and who has dark hair and round breasts, takes singing lessons from my father. A retired seaman with a cap, a Bible and Baptist beliefs, either a friend or family of her mother's, offers us his newly built house for rent at a reasonable price.

Daily life takes on an appearance of normality. My father earns just enough with his music and his job as a textile salesman to keep the heads of our extended family above water. Without the sale of jewelry from better days, life would have been austere indeed. My school life which had been interrupted is now resumed. The rupture after the events in Rotterdam seems to be repaired. The teacher and my classmates accept me with friendliness, and cramming for the high-school entrance exam is more pleasure than pressure. For a short time, I taste youth. In another class, there's a slender girl with auburn hair and freckles who doesn't know that my thoughts are centered on her so much. My beret elicits a cooing and a giggle from her and her girlfriends. At home, I try to close myself off to the endless news reports, Hitler's hoarse bellows and the pessimistic analyses that follow. There are heated discussions at our table, during which Feiner's prophecies that the war will be over in three months are scoffed at by the members of my household and the many new émigré guests. The graying Dr Abel, philosopher and dentist, impoverished, wise and gentle, soothes the prickly atmosphere, takes a walk with me and tells me about the expanding universe.

My mother works her fingers to the bone, sometimes standing with her head bent to one side, listening with a resigned smile, sweeping back a strand of visibly graying hair with her wrist. My father often withdraws to the bedroom around nine o'clock, tired, unable to cope with the tension any longer.

A morning in May 1941, a clear blue sky, gleaming dew on the bushes; I'm on my way to the forbidding, hundred-year-old building that houses the public high school, where I am to subject myself, along with other boys and girls my age, to the entrance exam. Dr Logemann, the elderly man with gray hair, a searching gaze and creaking shoes who receives us in the bare classroom with its wooden floor, scratched desks and a huge black pot-bellied stove, fills us children with fear and awe. After the relative security of elementary school, we feel the seriousness of "society" and realize that a lot depends on the exam. Bent over our questions, always harder and longer than expected, we hear Dr Logemann's creaking step in front of, next to or behind us hour after hour. Sometimes a short silence falls. Then he looks over your shoulder but doesn't say a word and doesn't betray by a single gesture whether you're on the right track or not. No one even dares consider talking out loud or cheating.

If my memory doesn't deceive me, that exam lasted two days. In spite of the state of the war, the depressing rumors of roundups and the tensions in our overpopulated house, my parents, the members of my household and I awaited the result as if it were a valuable document. Such relatively small matters could loom very large on the horizon for a short while. We weren't left in uncertainty long. I appeared to have passed the entrance exam, but as Dr Logemann, the principal, more or less wrote, entrance was nevertheless denied because of an ordinance issued by the occupying force, which stated that Jewish children weren't allowed to be educated in non-Jewish institutes.

You can react to such situations in a variety of ways. My father chose an active response: he requested an appointment with Dr Logemann, who invited us to come to his home for a talk. There was an uncomfortable atmosphere at tea, during which it appeared that he had already taken steps to have a Jewish colleague, Dr Wijler, give me lessons in language and humanities. He himself would help if I had problems in math and science.

In the course of 1941, the political danger became more tangible as time went by. Fear of deportation and the future grew within families and one's circle of friends. The weekly lessons were a relief rather than a burden to me; an enchanted garden, to which fear had no access.

This routine was rudely disrupted by Dr Wijler's suicide. The words of a neighbor and snatches of a conversation from the half-open front door of his house made me numb with pain. This event must have been as shocking to Dr Logemann as it was to us. He continued to let me come to his home, even though this was potentially dangerous for him.

Arrests and deportations increased in the Netherlands in the spring and summer of 1942. Several families in Apeldoorn had already been affected. 2 October 1942, no later than about five in the afternoon, an hour at which you think: they won't come anymore today . . .

While awaiting further deportation, dozens of Jewish families, including mine, were locked up in the cells of Apeldoorn's police headquarters. The feeling of surprise and despondency that overpowers one in these circumstances can't be described. We sat there with many other people, but made little noise. I heard a door open and shut again. Footsteps came in our direction. Boots, but also other shoes, creaking. Dr Logemann stood at the door to our cell. Older, gentler, having trouble holding back his tears. A math book in his hand: "Take this with you, maybe you can still do something over there. They let me come and wish you bon voyage."

THE ILLUSIONISTS

The registered package the size of a hardback textbook with the German National Archives as the return address lies like a hot brick in my hand. I know what its menacing contents are without opening it. A few weeks prior to this, my suspicion that the film still exists and that the archives in Koblenz possess a videotape was confirmed. Several historians, including the Dutch historians Presser and De Jong, knew about its production, but believed that the film I now hold in my hand was lost.

I requested it for educational purposes, but the scholarly motive is only a cover for my anxious curiosity. I stand there, in the safe environment of my institute, with the fragment of a movie entitled *Der Führer schenkt den Juden eine Stadt* (Hitler Has Given the Jews a City), which was filmed at the cost of the lives of more than seven thousand Jews in the Theresienstadt camp between 16 August and 11 September 1944. Amidst the dozens of empty tables and chairs in a lecture room bleakly lit by fluorescent light, I put the videocassette in the VCR with cold, unsteady hands, switch on the monitor and, with temples pounding, await the first image.

The Offenbach overture booming from the loudspeaker assails the senses like a box on the ears and is accompanied by pictures of the metal workshop in which half-naked men forge glowing iron on anvils to the tempo of the music. The shrill voice of the German commentator: "To maintain and replace various kinds of machines and equipment, a series of workshops employing smiths, metalworkers, mechanics and electricians is indispensable. Workers from a variety of trades and occupations can carry on their work in Theresienstadt."

The music of Jewish composers, already banned in Nazi Germany and the occupied territories for years, continues. The voice follows the images with empty propaganda: arts and crafts, a sculptor with his design for a fountain, workshops in which women and men plaster smiles on their ashen faces on cue and, wearing the Star of David on their chests, repair shoes, cut out purses and sew clothes to the vigorous sounds of Mendelssohn's *Midsummer Night's Dream*. The *Feierabend* ("free" time after work) and the game of football with two times seven instead of eleven players in the courtyard of the Hamburg barracks, with thousands of extras in badly fitting clothes hanging over the balustrades; stage-managed enthusiasm. A bathhouse with men standing under showers from which, in Theresienstadt, only water comes. A library in which Prof David Cohen[8] sits behind the check-out desk with a smug expression on his face and converses with a colleague. A speech by Prof Utitz, with the audience consisting of dozens of internationally renowned Jewish scholars, reduced to emaciated old men in their carefully smoothed down but worn-out suits, with bent glasses in front of mournful eyes and stars over their angst-filled hearts.

A fragment of a concert. The conductor, Karel Ançerl, standing in front of a string orchestra comprised of the best string players in Europe. These musicians had been driven from concert podiums with the tacit consent of conductors who thought they could save art by making a pact with the devil. The first performance of a *Fantasy for Strings* by Pawel Haas, composed in captivity somewhere in a dark attic in Theresienstadt, on gray waste paper on which the young pianist Gideon Klein had drawn the bars. Despite the staged farce, some of the listeners appear to soar above the agony of their imprisonment for a moment.

Then the picture jumps to the carefully tended vegetable gardens where a group of predominantly young people are weeding and watering the plants to the cheerful sounds of the music of the damned. The voice of the Nazi commentator Lampl: "In the family garden plots, there is always something to weed and water, and the produce is a welcome addition to the menu." The scenario neglects to mention that the gardeners incurred solitary confinement and deportation for eating these vegetables. On the other hand, there are shots of an idyllic summer evening, with women and children playing, talking, knitting. One mother is reading to her daughter. I recognize the girl: she survived the camp.

No staccato German voice in the last picture. A quiet supper, with an elderly gentlemen at the head of the table: David Cohen, actor to the last. The fragment of film is over. Flickering black and white on the monitor. Motionless, chilled to the bone, I stare into my past: the images of my own film pass in front of my eyes.

I see the shuffling men and women, shoving and hurrying one another, their faces ashen and tired, their steaming damp clothes, wrinkled, stained, worn out. The elderly, numb with cold, their backs bent, sometimes carrying a stick or a crutch, are passed up or inconsiderately thrust aside by youngsters and children on whose faces resignation hasn't yet settled, with hard eyes that already know too much.

I'm walking in this human stream through the long passages of the Hamburg barracks. With unsteady steps and the light dizziness of someone recuperating after a lengthy illness, I shuffle along with the old folks, urged to greater speed by men with armbands on their arms and old snow caps on their heads.

Because of loose or missing tiles and boards, the floor is uneven. Weather-beaten walls and worm-eaten beams from the time of Maria Theresa graze my shoulder. Arches and massive balustrades, worn smooth, open onto a courtyard, grayish-black with mud and half-melted snow. As in a sixteenth-century performance of a Shakespeare tragedy, there are thousands of people there, jostling one another against the parapets of the various floors. Leaning over each other in dense rows, their necks outstretched, a hand cupped behind an ear, eyes staring intently in the direction of the entrance gate.

A shout of something not quite audible comes from somewhere or other. Orders like "*Mützen ab*" (Caps off) and "*Ruhe*" (Quiet) spread like wildfire through the tangle of people. The pushing and shoving halt abruptly. Four men come through the gate. The first two in SS uniform, stiff but with a nonchalant arrogance. They stand to the right of the entrance, their backs to the building. Like disinterested, half-amused theater directors, they watch the entrance of the court jesters who come in after them in their dark overcoats and march clumsily to the middle of the courtyard.

I recognize one of them, and judging by the slight relaxation around me I feel the others do as well: Dr Wachtel, short and erect, with curly gray hair and the reassuring face of an old man, famous as the head of the *Antragstelle* (Application Department) in Westerbork, where he did his best for many people, even managing to procure a postponement in the deportation to the East for some of them. One of the few with a reputation for integrity, a rarity in a situation in which almost everyone who didn't belong to the transport proletariat landed up in the gossip and slander circuit.

Next to him, likewise small in stature, but at least twenty-five years younger, with the carefully groomed appearance of a Berlin University professor still almost intact, Dr Eppstein, Jewish Elder of Theresienstadt. We knew nothing about him except that, if the rumors were true, *Hauptsturmführer* Rahm, the newly appointed camp commandant, the taller of the two uniformed spectators, sometimes snapped at him and even hit him in public.

Wachtel and Eppstein stood there in the middle of the inner courtyard, bearers of an unknown message that was awaited with both dread and hope. The focus of thousands of eyes. The Jewish Elder spoke, but only a few could understand him well. His voice didn't carry and the fragments of the sentences that penetrated the uneasy wall of silence gave the impression of a standard speech uttered mechanically. We should be grateful we had come to a "privileged" concentration camp like Theresienstadt. We were to show ourselves worthy of this honor by our correct attitude, industry, cleanliness and discipline. The valuables and money that had been intentionally or unwittingly not turned over on arrival were to be handed over immediately. Failure to do so would result in solitary confinement and deportation; and more rules, rules, rules.

Our attention flagged. The air was abuzz with whispers. We had already learned a thing or two: one or two years' camp experience in Westerbork or Vught had left its mark on us. Only one question was burning in our brains: were we safe from deportation to the unknown, menacing East? Dr Wachtel understood our agony. Total silence fell when he uttered his first words. Speaking deliberately and clearly, in a southern German accent and with the practiced voice of a former officer, he pronounced the words that extinguished the fire of our burning concerns: he, an ex-officer of the 1914–18 war, awarded the Iron Cross First Class and the Order of Merit, had been assured by Commandant *Hauptsturmführer* Rahm, on the word of an officer, that we, the transportees from Holland, would be allowed to stay in Theresienstadt, provided we behaved ourselves.

In the middle of May 1944, four months after these words had been uttered in good faith, we had the opportunity to ponder our gullibility during the three days and two nights we spent in sealed boxcars en route to our destination: Auschwitz-Birkenau.

The arrival in Hades has been described many times, and I try to smother the flames that leak through the safety curtain of my memory by keeping it closed.

Several hours later, I find myself together with my father in the area behind Crematorium III, whose function I didn't know, nor would I have been able to comprehend even if I had known. We are standing or sitting on hard, black ground, stripped of everything except our rumpled, travel-stained clothes, searching in the mass of people for family, gasping for water, waiting like cattle before the slaughterhouse. Any awareness of time has vanished. In the distance, men with hardened faces, striped pajama tops and berets are dragging pieces of baggage. SS men don't mix with us, but are clearly visible in the watchtowers behind their black, gleaming machine guns.

One of them calls out something below, in Dutch: "Are you from Holland?" The proverbial straw, an omen?

In the dewy semi-darkness of the dawn, we're herded together by prisoners in striped uniforms carrying truncheons. There are a few SS men among them, like farmers driving their livestock and dogs. I see my mother and feel I'm alive again. In columns of five, we walk over a stony road, between two rows of concrete posts strung with barbed wire and white porcelain insulators. To the right are several gates with inscriptions, illegible in the dark. Behind them are stone buildings and long barracks, endless rows.

At the next to last gate, our column veers to the right. A long road dissolves in the darkness. First, we see two crude brick houses on either side of the street and then countless stables, their doors opening on to the Lagerstrasse. A prisoner shouts in a hoarse voice, a broad-shouldered hunchback dressed in stripes with an armband around his arm and a heavy club in his hand, then chases us cursing and ranting into one of the stables. I see my father but can't reach him in all the tumult. A raised brick walkway stretches across the entire length of the barrack, a foot and a half high and just as wide, over which striped figures with truncheons walk back and forth, shouting like lion-tamers, beating on heads, backs and the corner bars of the three-tiered sleeping platforms.

Then an order is given and total silence falls. I stand as still as a statue, my eyes fixed. A *Blockführer*, in field green and carrying a walking stick, marches past with the *Blockälteste*, inspecting or counting. Further away, I hear dull blows but remain as frozen as the men around me. After fifteen minutes: "*Weitermachen*" (Carry on). The statues come to life. The herd is now driven along the registration tables.

On these tables: paper, ink, pens. But how different and frightening the use of these simple writing implements is. One striped figure notes our names and other relevant information and calls out a number, and the second grabs my left arm and rapidly tattoos a letter and a number. From now on, I am A–1321. Many people have their number crossed out with the needles and replaced by another. The administrative competence of the tattooers can be read on our arms. Every prick burns in our brains, and woe be unto he who does not know his new "name" perfectly.

Orders and blows descend on us like fickle showers. We're mere specks of dust blown from place to place. No corner is safe, no step goes unnoticed. Everything is accompanied by hoarse shouts and arbitrary beatings: wiping the eternally muddy floor with old rags, lugging overfull barrels to the cesspool at a quick march, fetching kettles of scalding watery soup, tidying our beds made of fraying horse blankets and leaking paper mattresses, washing ourselves with hundreds of others at one dripping faucet, waiting to the point of exhaustion in perfectly straight lines for our bread and a spoonful of inedible soup, undergoing lice checks of clothing and hair, attaching triangles and numbers to our clothes, being awakened and having to line up in the dead of the night.

One day is tacked on to another in endless dullness and resignation. Work doesn't bring any regularity either. People who just happen to be standing next to each other are barked at by a Kapo or a *Blockälteste* and prodded into a quick march. Seconds later, they're pushing overloaded wheelbarrows, shoveling sand, scrubbing latrines or sweeping the dusty camp roads. After the evening count, my father and I look for my mother among the countless mothers in the women's barracks. Often to no avail. Then the day ends in the morass in which it began. Sometimes, we find each other and exchange words choked with tears, almost ashamed. What's there to say that she doesn't know or fear?

There's no language in the hell to convey what I see, hear, smell or taste. Terror and dread have cordoned off my emotions. I smell the stench of decay and oily smoke, but don't understand. I see and hear the trains, the stumbling masses of people en route to the flames, the dull blows, the naked and shorn women, their private parts exposed, three of them crouched under one gray rag, dripping rain water, but I don't understand. Night and day, my senses record what's happening on the other side of the barbed wire and the watchtowers on the "Ramp" and in the neighboring sections of the camp, but I don't understand.

Who are they, the others? We have hair and clothes, are hungry but not starving to death, have Kapos who hit but seldom aim to kill and we can exchange words with relatives. One rumor has it that there's a Children's Block where milk and bread are distributed. Things are bad where we are, very bad, but all around us are things I can't comprehend, where the word "bad" no longer has any meaning. Fischer, the *Lagerkapo*[9], a monstrous bundle of muscles and hoarse roars, always swinging his club in his hands or letting it dance over our backs, pours out a torrent of abuse, prophesies gas and the chimney, the end of our suffering. His words continue to ring and are countered by our will to survive. Compound B II B, the "Family Camp," seems to be a reserve where it's forbidden to beat the bushes, but where game may be thinned out and shot.

It wasn't until July 1944 that it dawned on me that our "unique" position was a sham and a lie. Words tossed out, picked up and sometimes passed on string themselves together into rumors: selection, *Blocksperre*,[10] Schwarzhuber,[11] liquidation, Mengele,[12] work transport. The beginning of the summer brings an end to every illusion. The wail of sirens and Kapos sends us into the barracks. The *Blockälteste* and his helpers herd us, that is boys under sixteen and men over forty-five, to the end of the room. We're not worth selecting from.

The men between sixteen and forty-five march naked past Mengele, their left arms in front of their chests. A few yards in front of him is a pole over which they have to jump. Recruits in a gymnasium. The signs he gives to the clerks are barely perceptible. The *Blockführer* snaps at a man who doesn't show his number clearly enough. A few times, Mengele leans slightly forward in his seat at the table to take a better look at a foot, a hand, a scar. The last group is chased past him at a fast pace. The clerks are having trouble keeping up. The *Blockälteste* relegates the weak, the wounded, the emaciated, the limping and the bespectacled, the rejected fallen fruits, to the corner of the useless with a short jerk of his head.

An order makes us freeze in position. The SS men leave the block. Tumult is stifled by blows. In the silence, the numbers sound like death sentences to those not named. I don't see my father, but I hear his number. He has to leave me behind. Whatever strikes my retina in this chilling hour barely touches my emotions. One question races through my head: what are they doing with my mother?

The *Blocksperre* ends with the shofar scream of the siren. Fragments of sentences about mothers, friends and relatives descend on us like driftwood in a waterfall. There were other selections elsewhere in the Family Camp. The women's blocks can't be reached because of a cordon of Kapos and their helpers.

Someone, unknown, faceless calls my name and brings the message of my damnation: "Your mother is being transported, her number has been called."

The days after the selection have lost their meaning. My "self" has passed away, my shadow has disappeared. In the week that follows, I mechanically do what I'm ordered, lug straw mattresses, scrub floors and stairs, drag barrels of excrement and try to get through to the transport blocks without being observed.

I find my father, mute, staring in fear or resignation, almost a stranger.

July 9th brings a pale-blue sky, a merciless sun and sandy flurries of wind. The first wail of the siren ending the *Blocksperre* pierces my lethargy. I quickly find my father. The doors of his barrack are still open. Breathless, I force him to go with me. A cordon has already been formed around the women's barracks, but there is still a way in around the back, by the wire. I run crouched low across the open areas between the blocks, looking for cover against the rear wall or the doors. I expect shots, but they don't come. My father stays behind and hesitates to cross the open field. I run up against the cordon. A striped figure raises his club menacingly, changes his mind and signals me to get out of sight.

Half hidden behind the stable door, I see them standing there. In rows of five, not yet at attention, hundreds of women waiting in silence with expressionless faces, wearing their own crumpled clothes, with scarves on their heads. My eyes devour the rows until they come to a halt by my mother's knitted, grayish-blue, wool-blend jacket, the coat that I, as a nine-year-old boy, was allowed to help choose on another planet. My gaze cries out to her and her heart hears me. The seconds that we see each other, with tears that may not be, last an eternity.

The SS comes from the Lagerstrasse. The women are shouted to attention. We lose each other. The striped figure gives me an urgent sign and threatens me with his club. The others who likewise tried to catch a glimpse of the departing run back to their blocks like wounded animals in a forest fire. I see my father's ashen, tear-stained face. Our farewell is shared grief.

The door to my barrack, the one on the side by the wire, is

locked one second after I've wriggled through it. Something
has changed there. It's not so crowded, the sound is different.
Shouts have made way for moans, cries and sobs, for whispers
and prayers. Men are standing between the beds and against
the walls. Their heads covered, a rare few with a yarmulke,
their eyes closed, bowing and rocking back and forth:
Kaddish.

Others, sitting or lying on the bed boards which are no
longer so closely packed, are holding their heads in their
hands. One or two are howling like dogs.

I attempt to choke back my tears in silence, until a white-
haired man with a friendly wrinkled face pats me on the head
and talks to me. Then my control gives way to a flood of tears.

Dr Da Silva's solace doesn't reconcile me to my approaching
death and abandonment. He's grieving for his son, who's been
transported like my parents, but he's also optimistic about his
son's chance of survival. I saw their farewell and feel envious.
The tears are bitter.

My resignation slips away from me and gives way to unease.
Irritated, I brush past the praying and the desperate in search
of boys my own age. It's as if we're looking for each other and
find what we're searching for. Faces from Westerbork and
Theresienstadt: Jan S., Sieg F. and Günther M. We have no
words. We don't accept death. Jan S. suggests talking to the
Blockälteste and disappears between the old men, whom he
refers to as "*Muselmänner.*"[13] His tenacity gives us hope, but
when he stays away a long time, it fades again.

I see him returning, his face a question mark. Before he's
even back among us again, the stable door is flung open. The
Blockführer's stocky figure is outlined against the glaring

daylight. Even before everyone comes to attention and freezes, he gives an order like the crack of a whip: "*Alle Jungs raus!* " (All boys: outside!). At that moment, I know that I will live.

What happens to us outside escapes me somewhat. The transition was so sudden. I see dozens of youngsters my age, many who are shorter, several my height; most of them have the thin bodies of city-dwellers, but a few have the firm muscles of farm boys.

What do you have to look like in order not to be sent from the line? I tense my muscles, breathe deeply to expand my chest and run past Buntrock[14] and Schwarzhuber. I nearly stumble. An incomprehensible remark is flung at my head, but I'm allowed to line up with the other boys.

We can't share our fear and insecurity. Words get caught in our throats and our eyes set rigidly in their sockets. Hundreds of boys in rows of five are waiting for something and someone, for some kind of change. Mengele arrives in the square for roll-call on his bicycle. I don't understand what he and Schwarzhuber say to each other, but suddenly he's standing in front of us, looking us over like a farmer inspecting his livestock. He questions the short and the tall, who jump to attention like soldiers on drill. With every rejection, I stand straighter, my fists at my side, my head made of granite. He walks past and leaves me alone.

In columns of five, we march up the Lagerstrasse, the cattle-drivers with their prods next to us, untrained recruits who know that any slip can cost them their lives. We're called to a halt next to the emergency water reservoir near the fence. Buntrock, the *Blockführer*, walks along the rows and counts. I hear him swear at a small boy with a non-Jewish face at the end of the column. For a moment, it looks like he's going to hit him and send him back. Then the unprecedented happens: the boy says something, pleads with the SS man, who feints a kick and shouts "*Abhauen*" (Beat it) to him and the rest of the column. Otto stays with us: a good omen?

We're counted again as we go through the gate. The walking stick goes up and down at every fifth row. And then we march toward the sun, which sharply outlines the silhouette of the crematoria against the pale-blue sky.

To the right and the left is the electrified barbed wire, like guide lines in a perspective drawing. Everything is clearer now than it was two months ago, when, in semi-darkness, I landed in this hell.

Now, en route to the unknown, I feel a hundred years older. My fatalism is pierced by stabs of panic. Are we really going to Men's Camp B II D or are we marching toward the gas?

Hope fades when we walk past the gate of B II D. Fear stiffens our joints. A striped figure walking alongside the column notices the change in our rhythm and says in Yiddish, without turning his head: "So you *are* headed for the sauna." We veer to the left and before long are standing in a steamy room with clothes hooks on the walls.

Stocky striped figures with gleaming shaved craniums take charge of us. We undress under threats and oaths and an occasional beating. I try to put my shoes in a place where I can find them again, the shoelaces tied to each other. The razor scrapes cruelly across my lower abdomen. Our pubic hair and the hair from the heads of some of the boys falls to the floor. On a sign on the wall, I read "*Eine Laus, Dein Tod*" (A louse means your death). Our shame dies. Even the order "*Bücken und Arsch hoch*" (Bend over with your ass in the air) doesn't matter any more. Only the fear of pain remains.

We enter the showers and hear the bath Kapos utter their crude jokes about gas or our physiques. We try to remain passive. By making the water ice cold or scalding hot, the Kapos are able to prolong their enjoyment a little longer.

Suddenly, it seems as if the initiation ceremony is over. The grayish-blue striped uniforms and berets that the clothing Kapos toss to us give me a strange feeling of security. We swap for better fits and all at once look like real prisoners.

With the setting sun at our backs and our faces directed toward the endless rows of barracks, watchtowers and concrete posts with insulators and barbed wire, we march to Men's Camp B II D. The ritual counting of prisoners is repeated. I move my eyes warily to avoid having my glance cross that of an SS man or a Kapo. Something about the new situation dawns on me as I look at the faces of the older, booted or better-dressed prisoners: you can only survive here as a wolf among wolves.

Overcome by exhaustion and fear, I walk mechanically in the column to our new quarters. Passing through the gate in the wall that connects various blocks, we arrive at the yard between two barracks. A roll-call square: in front of the washroom to the left is a wooden saw-horse, a menacing construction used for flogging; to the right is Block 13, where the hard-labor gang is housed.

Shouting terse orders, a heavyset prisoner chases us through the side door. In the seconds that pass before the opening accommodates us all, I look around me. Muscular, tanned prisoners, their naked torsos tattooed all over with tanks, artillery, pennants and birds and their bald pates gleaming, are talking; some are shaving one another, their heads and faces full of soap, while others are sitting in a circle concentrating on an invisible game: Russians. A few sneak a look at us, but don't give any sign of interest: old monkeys in a monkey colony. Inside the barrack, the *Stubendienst*[15] is waiting for us, less hostile than I'd feared. The room, the bunks, the brick walkway running down the entire length of the barrack, over which only the big shots are allowed to walk, everything's the same as in the Family Camp. There's only one striking difference: order and cleanliness. Unsoiled straw mattresses that still have straw in them, no sick or dying prisoners and blankets folded with precision in straight lines.

We're assigned places to sleep and try to find familiar compatriots as bunkmates, but are snapped at when we're too slow.

The stable door is flung open. A stocky, broad-shouldered prisoner with his hair slicked back, his striped uniform freshly ironed and a truncheon in his hand, a "Red Triangle,"[16] crashes in, flanked by his helpers: Emil Bednarek, the *Blockälteste*. We stand at attention in front of the beds, without moving. He walks over the mid-section with big strides. He stands still, examines us, snarls something. There is absolute silence as he delivers his speech about order and cleanliness, cleanliness and order, industry and honesty, and the severe punishments if they are not maintained.

That evening, a leaden sleep confers oblivion on me until a whistle and the dull beating of truncheons against the bars of the beds at four o'clock in the morning toss me back into our drab misery.

Once the carriers of the kettles with the hot bitter liquid are inside and we have washed this breakfast down our parched throats, three to a bowl, I hear outside the whistle for roll call and the orders "*Antreten, Raus!*" (Fall in: outside!). To our surprise, we're not chased outside, but are lined up in front of the bunks. The *Stubendienst* shouts and counts. A *Rapportführer* (Reporting Officer) inspects us cursorily, counts under his breath and disappears as quickly as he's come. I catch the word "quarantine," but don't understand. Which one of us is sick?

Several older prisoners appear and order us to stand in front of the beds. Their lessons in how to make beds, scrub and sweep floors, stand at attention and salute, address and report to superiors are exhausting because they are endlessly repeated and bellowed with cynical scorn by the instructors. They're hard and tough, but not totally devoid of all feeling. They ask where we come from, sometimes our names, but gruffly parry counterquestions. A wall of determined silence.

After the evening roll call, which almost passes us by unnoticed, I see one of them again when bread is being passed out. The words "Family Camp" fall like a smoldering spark. Unexpressed and inexpressible questions race through me, and I see in the staring eyes of my companions that they're tormented by the same thoughts.

Less than two hours later, I'm lying on my back on the straw mattress and staring into the darkness, listening to the night. I feel that all around me dozens of pairs of eyes are trying to pierce the darkness and, outside, above the sounds of sleep, I can hear the rumbling screech of trucks. A single dull shot, like fireworks set off in the fog. Vague shadows of yellowish-orange flames glide along the barrack's transom windows.

When the day begins at four a.m., night falls. The sky is black. Wordlessly, like shadows of ourselves, we glide through the next twenty-four hours. The older prisoners spare us with words. The second night is like the first, but sharper, clearer.

After roll call, our quarantine is lifted. Of the seven thousand who remained in Birkenau B II B, there's only smoke and ashes. Their *Sonderbehandlung* (Special Treatment) has been completed. The Family Camp has been liquidated.

* * *

The Danish King Christian X has gone down in contemporary history as a man of great moral courage. His threat to be the first to adorn himself with the yellow Star of David if the Danish Jews were ordered to wear this badge kept the Germans from carrying out the measure. This attitude, displaying great strength of character in June 1942, was not an exception. Rather, it typified the mentality of the entire Danish bureaucracy and the population toward National Socialist Germany.

This attitude did not fit in at all with the racist thinking of the Nazi leadership in Berlin. In their eyes, "outstanding Aryans," as they viewed the Danes, would automatically accept the Nuremberg Laws and the deportation of the Jews. However, nothing was farther from the truth.

The RSHA[17] and von Ribbentrop[18] gave the German plenipotentiary in Denmark, Dr Werner Best, to understand that he had better prevail upon the Danes to cooperate in the "Final Solution to the Jewish Question." Best anticipated great difficulties and feared strikes and sabotage which might especially endanger the enormous deliveries of food to Germany. In a personal conversation held in August 1943, Hitler demands that Best press on with the preparations for deportation.

On 29 August, the Danish Army is disbanded and interned by Wehrmacht General Hannecker. The Scavenius government steps down and leaves the ruling of the nation in the hands of the civil service. These civil servants likewise reveal great moral rectitude.

Preparations are finalized, and when Hitler decides on 18 September 1943 that the Danish Jews have to be deported, these plans are made operational. The German Naval Attaché, G.F. Duckwitz, immune to Nazism, leaks the plans on 28 September to Hans Hedtoft, later Denmark's Prime Minister.

And then an underground lightning operation of resistance and aid unparalleled anywhere in Europe begins. Copenhagen's Chief of Police makes unauthorized use of the broadcasting system to warn the populace. The police refuse to cooperate with the Germans in any way, and within two days, six thousand Jews from Copenhagen and the surrounding areas are provided with a hiding place.

When the morning of 2 October 1943 dawns, the *Grüne Polizei* [19] has captured only 477 persons, for the most part older people.

Sweden is also involved in the rescue operations, probably through King Christian. The Swedish representative, Von Dardel, promises asylum to any and all Jews who cross over to

Sweden, giving the green light to hundreds of nighttime crossings in fishing boats during the month of October. All conceivable forms of aid are given from all strata of the Danish population, with the Danish police overseeing the safety of the Jews and their helpers. At the end of October 1943, 5,919 Jews, 1,301 half-Jews and 686 non-Jewish spouses have eluded their persecutors.

The reception of the captured Danes in Theresienstadt at the beginning of October resembles a farce. Dr Eppstein, the Jewish Elder, is ordered by Burger, the SS Commandant, to give them a gracious reception, with an excellent meal awaiting them on nicely laid tables. Burger, his assistant Haindl and a few SS men serve as charming hosts, and when everyone is sitting somewhat reassured at the table, one or two even smoking, they distribute postcards and request the Danes to inform their friends in Denmark of their safe arrival and pleasant experiences, then discreetly absent themselves. Once the cards have been collected, the tableau changes abruptly: they are obliged to hand over money and valuables and sew on yellow Stars of David under the threat of corporal punishment and solitary confinement, and the billeting begins.

In the months to follow, it appears that the Danish group is clearly given preferential treatment in the camp. Clothing left behind in their hurriedly vacated dwellings (which were protected by the Danish government) is forwarded to them, their accommodation compares favorably with that of the other prisoners and well-filled food packages, which the Danish and Swedish Red Cross sends to all the deportees from Denmark, even the stateless ones, are distributed relatively intact. This state of grace was incomprehensible to the ordinary mortal; a puppet show with impenetrable puppeteers in Berlin.

Immediately after the roundup of 1 October 1943, Christian X, despite being under house arrest, together with Danish diplomats, ecclesiastical dignitaries and other influential Danes takes steps to obtain permission from the German authorities in Copenhagen and Berlin for the Danish Red Cross to enter Theresienstadt.

To Eichmann and his colleagues, the request to visit the charnel house they had created must be an unwanted intrusion, all the more so because it comes from the land of grain and butter. Theresienstadt, death and transit station for Western European Jewry, rife with overcrowding, filth and human misery, first has to be put in order before Berlin will tolerate the visit of strangers.

Dr Mildner, still head of the *Sicherheitspolizei* and SD[20] in Denmark in 1943, is familiar with the Danish strength of character and persuades the head of the Gestapo, Müller, to allow an International Red Cross Committee into the camp. The German Red Cross, under the direction of *General-hauptführer* Hartmann, had already visited the "privileged" concentration camp Theresienstadt earlier at the request of the International Red Cross in Geneva, but Danish pressure opened the way to an International Red Cross delegation from Geneva.

In anticipation of 23 June 1944, the day the Red Cross Committee is to appear, the première of a deadly comedy is staged. Gogol's *Government Inspector* in a sham Potemkin village. The "beautification" of Theresienstadt requires

Gogol's pen to record its absurdity. Words fail to describe the cynicism of its organizers.

H.G. Adler and Z. Lederer give a report of the cleaning, the painting and the building of façades and model homes along the carefully mapped route the Committee had to follow; the furnishing of café and recreation areas; the relocation of the sick and unpresentable; the rehearsing of obligatory answers; in short, the countless matters required to orchestrate the grand delusion. The imprisoned extras, threatened with death and destruction, flawlessly build their own stage set, under the all-seeing eye of the SS. However, even the best sets cannot disguise the fact that every room, every dormitory and every barrack is a human warehouse filled to overflowing.

The "beautification" of Theresienstadt, destined from the time it was founded in 1941 to pull the wool over the eyes of foreign countries, has a grim beginning: the thinning out of the ghetto population. In the beginning of May 1944, few of the face-lift activities are visible to the deportees.

In the carpentry shop, the former indoor riding arena, where I daily cut out dozens of wooden soles on an old lathe, craftsmen make chairs, tables and other pieces of furniture intended to furnish the Potemkin village, under conditions of great stress. Feverish activity also prevails at the office of the Council of Elders. *Hauptsturmführer* Rahm, Burger's new successor, walks in and out, rants and raves and swears at Dr Eppstein and engineer Zucker, who are unable to put together fast enough the transport lists, which have to contain over 7,500 names. They are ready on 15 May 1944: 2,543 Czech, 3,125 German, 1,276 Austrian and 559 Dutch Jews who will do their bit for the "beautification" of the ghetto by being transported to Auschwitz. *Der Führer schenkt nicht allen Juden eine Stadt...*" (Hitler Hasn't Given Every Jew a City...) and most assuredly not the 1,200 unpresentable TB patients who are also included on the transport lists.

Until 1964, the year of the Auschwitz trial in Frankfurt, there was a shroud of mystery over the events in Family Camp B II B of Auschwitz-Birkenau. With a few exceptions, the small group of survivors had buried the horrors in the recesses of their minds or held their tongues behind bars.

We, the rejects from Theresienstadt, did not understand why our fellow inmates in the adjacent sections of the camp wore camp rags, had their hair shorn and were shot down or beaten to death in front of our eyes. Through the wire, we saw a hell that was even blacker than the portal of our own hell. But the older prisoners from the Main Camp Auschwitz I and the powerful *Blockältesten* and Kapos in Birkenau were also surprised at the special position of the "Family Camp." After all, they knew that immediately upon arrival, every transport underwent a selection on the "Ramp" and that all or the majority went up in flames. But the thousands who were driven away from the Family Camp in trucks in March and July 1944 only wound up in the gas chambers via the most circuitous of routes.

One of the leading witnesses in the Auschwitz trial, Dr Otto Dov Kulka, Professor at the Institute for Modern Jewish History at the University of Jerusalem, the small and courageous Otto in my story, looked in various European archives for an explanation of the puzzle of "Family Camp Birkenau" and found an answer in the correspondence between the RSHA and the German Red Cross, in Eichmann's memos and in the exchange of letters between the International Red Cross (IRC) and the German Red Cross (GRC).

Rumors about the mass exterminations in the East began to get through to the world in 1943. The IRC in Geneva put pressure on the GRC to inspect the camps. Niehaus, *Oberführer* of the SS, Eichmann's comrade and head of the Board of Directors of the GRC, urged the RSHA to create a "model camp" in Auschwitz that could hide the ghastly reality from the GRC and, if the worst came to the worst, from the IRC. The first transports from Theresienstadt which arrived in Birkenau in September and December 1943 overcrowded the Family Camp and were for the most part exterminated on 6 March 1944 in order to make room for the May transports from Theresienstadt, then in the frenzy of "beautification."

None of us suspected anything. After all, those arriving earlier had sent cards with positive and reassuring messages. In fact, the cards bore the date of 25 March, and their writers had already gone up in smoke three weeks before that.

The RSHA, particularly Eichmann and Günther, yielded to the pressure to allow the GRC and the IRC into Theresienstadt. In the meantime, Mildner had also managed to persuade the head of the Gestapo, Müller. Refusing Denmark, Sweden and Geneva would add to the distrust and heighten the risk internationally. The curtain was ready to go up on the "beautification" of Theresienstadt, and 7,500 people had to disappear in May 1944 behind the second stage set: the Family Camp in Birkenau.

On 23 June 1944, the IRC Committee appeared at the gates of the Potemkin village in Theresienstadt. Dr Rossel of the

Board of Directors in Genéva, F. Hvass, head of the Political Section of the Ministry of Foreign Affairs in Copenhagen, Dr J. Henningsen, the Danish Red Cross representative in Copenhagen, a doctor from the GRC and nine top-ranking SS officers walked down the predesignated route and talked to threatened prisoner-marionettes. Hvass and Henningsen distrusted the farce staged by the SS for Danish and Swiss eyes, but Dr Rossel was taken in. His naive report[21], dated a few days later, made the insistence of the IRC on more in-depth investigation superfluous.

Eichmann could breathe a sigh of relief. Auschwitz-Birkenau was spared the sight of prying eyes. The second stage set could be eliminated. It was burned the night of 10–11 July 1944.

The multicolored, eighteenth-century façades, the newly paved streets, the café, the Children's Home, the music pavilion, the display windows of nonexistent stores, in short, the stage set which was such a pleasant surprise to naive Dr Rossel from spotless Geneva, was too tempting to the SS top brass in Berlin and Prague not to exploit it for further propaganda purposes.

A film had to be made, one which would convince those at home and abroad of the humane treatment that was meted out to the Jews by the *Führer*.

The film was made. Thousands of imprisoned extras, who knew they were playing for their lives, were recruited. Kurt Gerron, a famous movie and cabaret star in Berlin in the twenties, directed as if his life depended on it. Jo Spier, the artist with all-too pliable a character, sketched the scenes and

František Zelenka, the stage designer from Prague, did the staging, supported by dozens of quasi-voluntary and quasi-coerced professional co-workers.

Like Hollywood movie producers, high-ranking SS officers, including Hans Günther, his brother, Eichmann's deputy and many more, came once or twice a week from Prague to play out their producer's role "on location."

During the weeks of the filming, between 16 August and 11 September 1944, Theresienstadt was a grotesque movie studio with spectators in black uniforms and caps with death head insignias commanding the movie-makers and actors and admonishing them to remember their mortality. The privileged artists believed themselves safe and indispensable. For two weeks, the black-uniformed illusionists of mercy kept the fantasy alive by granting gifts and favors. In the weeks between 28 September and 28 October 1944, 17,520 film-makers, actors and extras journeyed to the terminus that was Auschwitz. Only 1,496 returned. Kurt Gerron was not one of them. For services rendered, he was given Special Treatment with cyanide gas immediately upon arrival.

Almost forty years after this cynical comedy, the pictures passed before me with faces and buildings I recognized, but their incompleteness makes them alien. The long lines of hungry, begging and sick people, the filthy and overcrowded dormitories, the hearses crammed with cardboard boxes and pulled by bent old men, the gendarmes and SS men, but most of all the boxcars for transports to the East, remained invisible.

The movie was never released. All copies were destroyed.

Only fifteen minutes of celluloid lies were saved thanks to a clear-headed cameraman from Prague.

You can't fool all the people all the time.

LIBERATIONS

A chain of men in striped camp clothes winds its way over the slope of the gray-green hillside; one end of it disappears into the hazy forests. On my side, the row of skeletons draped in rags ends just before the narrow-gauge railroad track with its triangular dumpers. The explosions at irregular intervals in the stone quarries reverberate in our eardrums and empty stomachs, but today they sound as if they're at a safe distance.

Unlike yesterday and the weeks before that. Then we waited, exposed to the rain of rocks, at the redstone wailing wall perforated by dynamite holes and prayed wordlessly for protection. The brown shirts of the *Organisation Todt*[2] and the gray-green guards sought shelter before every explosion. We could only hope for chance and providence, but several times a day the bodies of our crushed comrades, whose suffering was at an end, gave lie to this hope.

This morning, I line up in another work squad and am pushed out of the line, but I doggedly persevere because I know that with my injured foot I won't survive another day in the quarry. The Kapos roar in the cold semi-darkness, yank on the columns and count. They drag and kick men like store dummies from work squad to work squad until the numbers tally. I'm still in my place.

We march over the stony road, stumbling, shuffling, scraping stone under wooden soles; stifled curses and suppressed cries of pain when a wooden clog is lost or broken. Guards with their guns on their shoulders, still sleepy in the early dawn. Wet with dew, the dented dumpers, reeking of rust and grease, await us. Grouped in clusters, we push and pull the dumper cars until we can no longer keep up with them and then jump on the sides and let ourselves be driven. Sometimes a jump fails, a clog slips off a foot, someone gets caught on something. He falls dozens of yards behind and, like a frantic traveler racing to catch the last train, runs to avoid falling into the hands of the guards.

We brake, try to pull him on to the side and let the flow of abuse from the Kapos and guards pass over us. They stand like generals on their chariots, egg us on, humiliate the clumsy.

We line up a few paces apart in the pale light of the sun, still hidden behind the edge of the woods, and form a human chain from the quarry to the railroad track. Boulders that bend our backs like wet reeds are handed from man to man to man and end with a thud in the metal bins. Our shadows shrink like the melting candles of our strength. Every time a link in the chain drops out, the load gets heavier. Those who fall stay where they fell. Nobody has the time or energy to move them aside. They ruin our chances; sympathy withers.

During the noon break, we tug at limbs and drag them to the railroad track. My legs are trembling, my chest is hollow, my head light. Everything is a dream. Hunger has lost its hold. Am I pulling or being pulled? While the guards brush the coveted crumbs from their field-gray uniforms, we form our broken human chain. The number of steps to the stone that I have to take from the arms of the man next to me has doubled. He sways like a lantern blown out in the storm and lets a boulder fall from his hands. Voices all around me, from far away and near by. German and Polish curses. The drumbeat of truncheons meeting flesh and the moans from our mouths. In a rosy haze, I try to lift the stone from the ground, but my fingers slide off the sandy, rough-hewn sides. It grows and seems to be rooted in the ground.

The voices fade away, a merciful silence. As if through clear water, I see the rolling landscape, a stream that fades into the blue-green woods on the horizon. My fall is painless. Blades of grass caress my cheek. Above me is the same landscape, unsullied by tears. I see myself escape my hunters with large, graceful bounds over fields and hills. My twin antlers are proudly outlined against the sky when I reach the other side of the stream, almost flying. My silhouette gets smaller and smaller, until it's swallowed up by the embrace of the far off forest. I feel freedom as I'm enfolded by darkness.

Untold hours and days later, my eyes meet those of the man lying motionless next to me on the soiled straw. He stares at me expressionlessly. His eyes glow feverishly in their orbits, the surrounding skin transparent from the ravages of hunger. I don't understand the breathy sounds coming from the mouth which no longer closes. His fleshless hand gropes in the straw, finds the pockmarked bowl, but lacks the strength to hold it. The dull metallic sound of a kettle, the slosh of watery liquid and the sickly smell of "soup" dispel my apathy. I understand his searching gesture, take the bowl and hold it beyond the overhanging bed boards which block us from the kitchen Kapo's view. Trembling from weakness and the fear of spilling the liquid, I slurp my portion of soup. My dying comrade attempts to sit up but falls back and turns his head away. I haven't got the strength to support him, and the man on his left is already staring into nothingness.

Without a twinge of remorse, I keep on slurping. Later, when a disembodied hand proffers a piece of bread, I take my neighbor's portion as well, for he's gone to a place where food doesn't count anymore. From the land of the dead, he saves my life. I play this game of resurrection two or three times, but when only a few of my companions in the lower bunks are still alive, I flee this underworld, and with my last ounce of strength I hoist my lice-infected and scabies-ridden body to the upper bunk.

Like feverish dreams, rumors whisper through the night, interrupted by the death rattle of the dying and the coughs, cries, curses and moans of the living. The SS has supposedly mined the camp and will blow it up when they leave. It is said that the water is poisoned, that Hitler is dead, that the Russians are near. Even the dull booming of cannons comes from another world. Nothing affects me anymore. Fever has spread out a soft eiderdown bed for me, and I stare with sleepy contentment through the windows of my nursery.

Sharp cracks of machine-gun fire burst my dream. The window of my childhood is again the window of the barracks: four small, dirty panes. And behind that glass is liberation: six, eight, ten horse's hooves, blackish-brown coats, steaming nostrils, the booted legs of the cavalry. The door is flung open.

Through a veil of tears I see the round faces of soldiers peer around the corner like bashful boys. Events now tumble over one another, like a speeded-up film. The drone of army trucks replaces the clatter of horseshoes. German men and women wrap us like infants in gray blankets and lay us down with anxious care in the trucks, with horses snorting in the background. Young Russian soldiers with the friendly and astonished eyes of children look on, their rifles against their chests, calling to one another, occasionally helping. Submissively, like a small child, I let things happen and fall asleep in the truck, holding the bread I had been given like a teddy bear in my arms.

Lukewarm water caresses my skin. The wounds sting every time they come in contact with the Lysol-smelling soap with which a large female hand is carefully washing me. Her face remains blurred. I don't dare look at her, overcome with long-forgotten shame. Exposing my hideously emaciated body to strange eyes suddenly makes me afraid. A young Russian, his head shaved, is leaning against the green wall, a watchful bath attendant. The smoke from his Russian filter-tip cigarette cuts through the smell of disinfectant. The nurse lifts me out of the water. For a moment, I stand without any support and look at the rusty steel girders of the factory ceiling high above me. The ceiling starts to spin around me faster and faster. As I disappear in a whirlpool of oblivion, I hear the soldier's gun clatter against the stone floor and feel hands that don't let me fall.

As the days go by, I discover the world around me. The whitish white of the sheets and pillowcases, the softness of the eiderdown, the smooth feel of the rim of the cup and light, sweet-sour custard against my mouth, the filtered sunlight, the stiff apron of the nurse, her light-brown hair. The circle of my observations gradually widens.

The two comrades next to me, death heads in eiderdown frames, the curtains flapping in a May breeze, the sputtering motorcycles of round-faced Cossacks and, at night, the groans, screams and sobs of my fellow patients in the other wards. Yiddish, Polish and Hungarian sounds, from far and near. The nurse talks to me, softly: the other face of Germany. She feeds me bouillon, spoonful by spoonful, as if I were a small child. She awakes us from our afternoon nap and nervously straightens the sheets, and tries to have us sit on our bony, wound-covered backsides.

Three thickset Russians come clattering into the room. The medals on their officer's uniforms, beige-green with red collars, inspire confidence. One of them is a blonde woman with worried, light-blue eyes, a doctor, as evidenced by the stethoscope on her chest. She gives me and my companion on the left a thorough examination and, without saying a word, looks at my foot, writes something on a piece of paper and leaves it on the table for the nurse. She doesn't wake up the third man. Judging by the subdued voices and the glances of the other two, I guess that liberation has arrived too late for him. They leave the same way they came in.

The nurse's face relaxes and she asks me, almost cheerfully, what I would like to eat most. My knowledge of delicacies has faded. All I want is big quantities to alleviate my insatiable hunger, which I'm beginning to notice again. A "giant pudding" I hear myself say, and she promises to get me what I ask for.

A few days later, she sits on the edge of my bed and watches in amusement as I devour the sweet quivering structure, a portion big enough for six people. Gratitude opens my ears, and in the humming silence of the rest hour she tells me in a half-whisper how her life has been crushed by the war. Her parents' farm gone up in flames, her father killed by looters, the livestock stolen, her sister raped, her mother fled. She doesn't accuse my liberators, but her tears are bitter. I have no comfort to give. Against my will, I feel a confusing pity.

June 1945 smells of sun, grass and freedom in Upper Silesia. The outside attracts me, but is still terrifying; life without barbed wire is so unusual. Shuffling and unsure, I explore the surroundings of my sickroom: the patch of grass outside the window, the hall, the other rooms. My fellow-sufferers in or by their beds are strangers and yet familiar. We find ourselves again, step out of the shadow world and recognize each other as human beings. Some have made forays into Wüstegiersdorf and return with sacks of sugar, boxes of butter, sides of bacon, shoes and clothing from the SS warehouses being emptied by the Russians. Gleaners behind the mowers. The gluttony with which some stuff themselves proves fatal.

One of the stronger patients, of whom I'm half afraid, enters my room with alms of sugar and butter. Vehemently, the nurse pleads for abstention. It's hard for me to admit she's right. The next day, he visits me again and finds me alone. In a mixture of Yiddish and German, he proposes returning to Holland with me as brother or cousin. In return, he offers help and support. I hesitate and tell myself that freedom is being tainted by lies, but it's only at night, when insomnia releases the hidden images, that I know what's holding me back: he, this well-fed kitchen Kapo, is standing with two or three SS guards at the barbed-wire fence that serves to protect the kitchen from us. Next to him, there's a tall barrel containing slimy chunks. We, hungry bags of bones, wait at a distance, fearful but determined, hoping for food, any kind of food. He tosses a half-rotten pickle our way. The pack hurls itself upon it. A second, a third throw. Hunger and envy create a scuffle. We push our way toward the barrel. Then the SS men reach into the vat and pour the decaying vegetables on our heads and shoulders, and the kitchen Kapo joins in with their shouting and laughter. Their carnival show ends when we flee, stumbling and crawling, to our barracks, panicked by shots fired in the air. Two men remain lying in the square, at one with the garbage.

The sunny present returns in the morning. With great difficulty, the nurse finds some worn but clean civilian clothes that don't hang too loosely. The shoes I covet don't fit my bandaged foot. I repress my thoughts as I slip on the camp-style wooden clogs. In the stained mirror in the hall, a scarecrow stares at me from dark eye sockets. Dragging myself, I grope my way to the door of the hospital. Two green-uniformed Cossacks on motor cycles are too wrapped up in their vodka to notice me, let alone answer my first greeting.

A flower-studded meadow and a babbling brook draw me to the other side of the village's main street. I stand, my legs unsteady, on the loamy footpath, surprised at my own steps. The path disappears to the right in fields and trees. The first houses of Wüstegiersdorf are on the left. Without barbed-wire borders everything seems to be infinitely spacious and far away. I feel like a toddler outside the garden fence and shuffle slowly in the direction of the open field where there's little chance of meeting someone. I stand still often and stare into the sun-drenched distance. My sense of oppression disappears and makes way for drunken happiness: free! I tire quickly and turn back.

A Russian soldier with a crooked kepi comes toward me with uneven steps, stands still in front of me and breathes alcohol into my face. The threat makes my legs shake. He points a fat index finger at my left arm and growls "*Uri.*" I shake my head and manage to answer fearfully "*No uri.*" He roughly bares my arm, sees the blue number and suddenly grins bashfully. "*Tovarich*" (Comrade), he shouts and rolls up his sleeve. No less than ten watches are ticking on his forearm. He unbuckles one of them, lays it in my hand and lurches on his way.

June is timeless. The days are divided according to food, the weeks according to recovery and weight. We talk about the past, our youth, our relatives.

"Where are you from?" "Where are you going?" The name of a camp is seldom mentioned; we don't have to tell each other anything. We wish to forget by day what we cannot forget by night.

My new friend from Debrecen is fading rapidly. TB colors his cheekbones red. He leaves the bed less and less frequently. His homecoming plans are wonderful. I don't dare express my doubts. The day the trucks drive up to the door to take those patients who are well enough to another building, a former Children's Home, he waves, weak and smiling, from his bed. My departure feels like desertion. I leave death behind me.

There's nothing childlike about the Children's Home. Old men, young in years, walk and totter around between the numerous white beds. We wait without knowing what we're waiting for and play with incomplete or homemade packs of cards and chess pieces to while away the time; we write, in the hope that someone is there to receive our letters; we quarrel about a shirt, a shoe or a sock while food is being served; we keep watch through the night; we sleep away the days.

The head of the Children's Home is Dr Goldstein, a small, stocky, active man, who takes his time with serious cases and is impatient with more straightforward ones. He wastes few words and doesn't appreciate replies. An unprotesting silence reigns when he's assigning patients to distribute food and act as nurse's aids and during his short speeches on rest and cleanliness. *His* black hair was never shorn. Sometimes he's away for hours and the rumor that he's leaving us to our fate races through the ward. Then he's standing in front of us once again, his bag full of bandages and medicines.

A few of the older, stronger, ones talk to him, first in the ward and then in the room next to the ward. They wish to leave, to go back to the places in Hungary or Poland that they had left years ago with their families in cattle cars. They pace up and down the ward, throughout the building. We ask them what's holding them back and their irritated reply makes us uneasy. "Goldstein won't give us a health certificate yet, the Russian Commandant is keeping us waiting for a pass, there's tension between the Polish and Russian troops, the Poles are closing the borders . . ."

In the warm last days of June, every morning a few more beds are empty. With or without papers, the men are leaving for the unsafe outside world that both tempts and terrifies us.

Reports from the village filter into the Children's Home. I know they're important, but don't feel they affect me. A world of grown-ups to which I don't belong. The Polish uniforms, occasionally visible from the window, mean nothing to me. What does the quarrel among the liberators have to do with me? I slowly realize that borders are being drawn; we won't automatically be able to pass through them.

Dr Goldstein is standing among the beds earlier than usual. More talkative and accessible, he announces the arrival of a Czech Red Cross bus which will take ambulatory patients to Prague. It's still uncertain whether the bus will be allowed through, but in case it comes, everything has to be ready. He reads aloud a list of names. Mine isn't included. At that moment I realize that I want to go too—to head home with them, to go in the direction of the Netherlands. I plead with my body, with my words. I can and will pass this selection. Troubled, he gives in and writes out my health certificate: "Certified to be without lice and typhus upon discharge" and promises to ask the Russian commandant for a pass for me.

When late in the afternoon a white bus with red crosses on the roof and sides stops on the playground, I'm ready and waiting, with a cane in one hand and a bundle of underwear and bread in the other.

We drive into the night. I can tell that the road is steep by the changing whine of the engine and the popping of my ears.

Condensation from our breathing forms a curtain over the dark windowpanes, but the world outside doesn't interest me. Hour after hour, the blackness glides by.

At Polish or Russian checkpoints, I sometimes emerge from my forgotten dreams for a few seconds and in the eerie light of the bus take my dozing companions to be trees felled by the wind. The moaning, gargling and mumbling sounds they make in their sleep are familiar to me: symphonies from hell.

The blackness outside the blank windows makes way for gray. We drive through empty villages, stretch our cramped limbs, guess at our destination. Vague questions begin to take shape in my mind. "Where are we going to stop, who will take us in, feed us, care for us? What lies ahead?"

The bus drives through a sea of houses as thin rays of sun drive away the gray. The city doesn't penetrate my cocoon. Our vehicle stops in front of a large gate. Our backs aching and our ankles swollen, we leave the bus and stand, unsteady and unsure, on the cobblestones of Prague.

A few people—ordinary people with ordinary, faded clothes, people from a world I had abruptly been forced to leave three years ago—lead us through the gate, through the corridor of an old monastery. They speak Czech, a few of them Hungarian. I don't understand, but feel their friendliness. My traveling companions inform me that we will be getting food and that accommodation is being sought. The sweetish aroma of fresh bread and the clatter of ladles against the sides of soup kettles inspire me with confidence. There's a chaotic pushing and shoving, and I'm the last to reach the serving point several minutes later. The fear of not getting anything grabs me by the throat. The woman with the white apron just manages to scrape up a full bowl of thick soup with peas. In a far corner of the monastery garden, I greedily spoon up my portion, my bread within arm's reach. The recent lesson was a hard one: I mustn't let my vigilance slip.

We've been blown apart like sands on a dune. My vocabulary is insufficient. No one speaks Dutch, German is tainted with blood or death and Yiddish rarely finds an understanding ear. I attempt to blaze a trail through the forest of incomprehension with Russian, French and English words. "A Dutch legation or consulate? Someone from the Red Cross?"

Serious, friendly faces nod no, until someone finally understands my uncertain search. We leave the monastery together. I walk next to him, my wooden clogs clacking painfully against my feet. He offers me his arm and tries in a laborious mixture of languages to tell me something about Prague, but the city roars in my ears and presses on my temples. Outside a large building he says goodbye and points to the gate. With a feeling of despair, I see him disappear between the houses.

The large old house threatens to call up the past: Theresienstadt. The copper plaque doesn't reassure me: Swedish Legation. I'm in the wrong place; he hasn't understood me, he's dumped me somewhere—they're going to let me rot! There's not a gatekeeper in sight. The door isn't locked, what can happen to me?

Even before I take in the scene, I hear snatches of Dutch, familiar sounds, life buoys. A short line of young men, some as shabby as I, are standing in front of a table in the middle of the courtyard. An older man is sitting behind the table, writing and asking questions. Next to him is a short, portly figure in a uniform I don't recognize. An officer in a bomber jacket. He leaves, saying goodbye: also a Dutchman.

The line welcomes me: "Where are you from, where have you been, how long, how bad?" The names of camps are passed back and forth like small change: "And your father; and your mother?" I'm overcome by emotion. I don't know if I have any tears.

I mechanically answer all the questions asked by the well-dressed man with the fountain pen. Five years pass before me like a bad dream: the bombardment of Rotterdam, the arrest in Apeldoorn, Westerbork, Theresienstadt, Auschwitz-Birkenau, Märzbachtal, Dörnhau, Schotterwerk. He writes and asks, listens to more than the words, gives me ration coupons for food and cigarettes and an address where I can sleep and promises me help and transport home.

André, a large blond-haired man from Delft, familiar with Prague after two years of resistance work and two years of camp, has come with some of his compatriots to pick up his ration coupons. He has listened with interest and offers to take me to the house where we are both staying.

A bumpy, rattling tram brings us to a street where there are large gray houses with damaged façades. A lot of rubble hasn't been cleared away yet.

"There was still some fighting here in April," André says. A different war than mine. How I would have liked to have fought here for my liberation. The place where I'm to sleep is a high and hollow room: austere and gloomy, with an iron bedstead and a chair. The matting on the floor reminds me of my room at home, long ago. There are no sheets. I fall into a bottomless sleep on the rough pillow.

The silence of the night awakens me. It rustles soothingly through the room. The choir of sighs and moans has fallen silent for the first time in years.

The next day, Prague looks kindly upon me. The houses no longer scowl. André helps me report to the police. My first official piece of paper. I'm once again someone with a name.

We eat in the Thomas Monastery, veterans without panic, but with ration coupons that give us rights. The journey to the legation doesn't seem as far as on the day of my arrival. Friends of André's are standing in the courtyard, and they greet me like an old friend. All around me the buzz of conversations about repatriation, transport and cigarettes. Light-hearted and joyful, I hand out my cigarette ration. Simply giving something away feels like freedom to me.

The man who had listened to my tale is the unassuming central figure, everyone's source of information. I hear his name mentioned: Hanepen. He arranges and takes care of things, talks with the Czechs in their own language, has contacts outside Prague. To everyone he's something of a genie, but no one knows exactly what his function is. He has managed to get transport to the West for my friends. In army vehicles heading for Pilsen, in the direction of Holland.

I nervously ask him if there's also a place for me. He looks at me solicitously: "If you really want to go, it might be possible." He considers it necessary to first consult another Dutchman, a doctor, to ask him to examine me, since the journey is long and arduous.

The fear of being left alone again drives me to feign good health, though my newly acquired friends advise against this transport. Hanepen makes a call and talks about me as if I were ill. Dr Polak Daniëls would like to see me tomorrow in his hotel on Wenceslas Square; "Don't worry, everything will work out all right." Scant comfort, but well meant.

I'm sure that I'll be left behind and roam disconsolately through the city on trams, standing on the platform. I get off anywhere, walk around a bit and sit on benches with old, silent men. No one says a word to me. Some people timidly avert their eyes, while others smile shyly, occasionally curious. I'm still wearing the sign of humiliation: my stubble-covered head.

Laboriously, I drag my heavy swollen feet along behind me. The left one won't let me forget what I want to forget.

Like fairy-tale magic, the Moldava is suddenly in front of me. Hradčany Castle, gleaming like gold in the full sunlight, towers tall and majestic on the other side of the river. I stand transfixed in front of the bridge with the apostles. Its beauty brings tears to my eyes, touches me for the first time in years and gives me a taste of freedom. My thoughts stray instinctively to the nameless Hungarian doctor who less than six months ago saved my life; I wish he were here with me on the Charles Bridge.

I lay on filthy straw in barracks in the Märzbachtal concentration camp, awaiting the end—living like a dog, my foot a dark balloon of blood and pus, my body an oven in the icy cold. There was nothing to distinguish him from the other prisoners. Except that his striped uniform was a bit cleaner. He pulls a package from his pocket, sets out two scalpels, motions me to put my foot on a stool.

Unbearable pain, which suddenly lessens once he's made

the incision. My foot gushes forth like a burst pig's bladder and I pass out. When I come to, he's sitting next to me. He has me swallow two pills, gives me some water and presses three more into my hand: "Don't forget to take them, they're my last Prontosil tablets."

How fervently I wish him to be alive, here, at the most beautiful place in Prague.

Although we both know that our paths will part, André wakes me up cheerfully and hurries me so that I'll be at Wenceslas Square on time. To my surprise, the doorman of the impressive hotel is polite and shows me the way to the "Holandski doctor." I recognize him in the doorway: the short, stocky, portly major who was in the courtyard when I arrived. He greets me loquaciously and orders real coffee, a long-forgotten luxury. He tells me about his escape to Switzerland, about his work here and about the Dutch people liberated from Theresienstadt. His words race past my head. Does he know why I'm sitting here? While he's drinking his coffee, I venture the question: has Mr Hanepen told him everything? I expect a check-up, but he only looks at my ankles and feet, shakes his head and requests a telephone call. In surprisingly rapid French, he talks to Henri, Colonel Henri, turns to me and asks: "Do you want to fly with the French to Paris?" Totally flabbergasted, I nod yes, without realizing what that involves. I drink my coffee, cold by now, and ask myself what lies ahead of me. He immediately dispels my anxiety and promises to pick me up in the morning and take me to the French Legation. They've agreed to take responsibility for me. I follow his narrative from afar, as my thoughts are focused on tomorrow. I don't have to say much, as he'd rather not hear camp stories.

My friends and I say farewell briefly and without much emotion. Our "we'll see each other in Holland" sounds as if that country is a market place in which you meet each other every morning in the café.

The night is long and my sleep troubled. I don't dare think about what I'll find at home, so as not to tempt fate. Images of Rotterdam, Apeldoorn, our last home, my parents, my aunt, the other members of our household, my dog pass before my eyes. While Prague is still slumbering, I'm ready to go, and I'm downstairs before Dr Polak Daniëls has switched off the engine of the dark green vehicle he calls a "jeep."

I miss much of what he says on the way to the French Legation. Uncertainty makes me deaf to the stories of others. His uniform, his words in French and the names he mentions open the gate and the doors. We wait inside for someone to fetch me. In the remaining minutes, Polak Daniëls gives me a present for the journey. He explains it to me: a "field ration" with chocolate and other precious food, full of calories, American.

Surprise and curiosity make the leave-taking less painful. As the young French officer takes me with him through the long corridor, we wave goodbye to each other as if we were family.

A silent man is seated behind a large desk in a spacious, high-ceilinged room. The only other furniture is a filing cabinet and a kitchen chair. The officer tells me to wait and says something to the man at the writing desk. I wait. The telephone rings constantly and people with files walk in and out. I'm still waiting. Prompted by hunger and inquisitiveness,

I open my package. I can't resist the profusion of chocolate, cookies, dried fruit and canned sardines, and I begin to eat, without restraint or remorse. I have eaten everything except the cans by the time the man turns around and notices me sitting there. Shy, I awkwardly ask when someone is going to fetch me, but I don't know if he understands. "Is something wrong? Can't I go with them? What can I do besides wait?" He bends over his papers again, as if I don't exist.

Finally a familiar face. The young officer comes in, sees me and swears: "Shit, we forgot you." He grabs my bundle of things in one hand and with the other drags me through the corridor, pushes me into the passenger seat of a black Citroën, jumps behind the wheel, screams something to the guards and races through the hurriedly raised barrier. Tires screeching, he tears around corners, and once I've caught my breath, I see the houses, streets and squares of Prague flash by to the blare of the horn.

The frightened giggle of a carnival ride comes over me, and when we screech to a stop at the airport, I step out of the merry-go-round of my childhood. A military plane with its propellers spinning is nearby. Men in overalls are standing next to the stairs, the rear door is still open. My escort waves and shouts. The men beckon. Once again, he pulls me like a rag doll behind him.

A clap on the shoulder is our farewell. I stumble up the stairs and with my head lowered disappear into the belly of the aircraft. I'm greeted by applause and a chorus of voices: "Bravo."

Before my eyes have adjusted to the darkness, many hands help me into a hammock. The door closes. The plane races at tremendous speed over the runway, there's a small bump and my ears feel blocked: we're flying to Paris.

Below me, a row of well-dressed French men and women are sitting next to one another on a long bench with their backs against the fuselage. They turn their interested faces toward me with a friendly laugh. We can't exchange very many words. Noise and a limited vocabulary get in the way, and yet I feel their sympathy.

The drone of the Dakota quickly lulls me into a deep sleep, from which I'm awakened by soft whispers and laughter. I feel a pressure on my legs, stomach and chest that I, half asleep, don't understand. When I open my eyes, I see the land of plenty. On top of me and all around me are chocolate bars, cookies, dried fruits, cans of sardines, nuts and merry faces. My voice hoarse with emotion, I stutter my gratitude, which is infinitely greater than they can ever know.

I can't hold back my tears at Le Bourget when many of them embrace me as we say goodbye. My face glows with the kisses of the women, young and old alike. I feel myself blush at this almost forgotten touch. One of the pilots helps me pack my riches and puts me in a Citroën like the one in Prague. On the paper that I give him is written "Centre d'accueil néerlandais, rue Leonardo da Vinci, Paris 16e": the address that Dr Polak Daniëls had given me at the time of my first cup of real coffee.

Paris glides darkly past the car windows. My attention is wholly taken up by the farewell. The Dutch Reception Center, in a large house called a hotel, is dark and closed; the reception is cool, distant. In a room with bunk beds, I find an empty straw mattress on which to sleep. Dinner was ages ago. I nibble at my rations, and when my fellow residents come in in their shabby suits, they show more interest in my goodies than in me. A heavy camp atmosphere hangs over the room, and before I fall asleep I hear words I'd rather not hear. The sunny Parisian morning doesn't permit any brooding. I have to go somewhere else in the city to report to a Dutch doctor, who can barely disguise the fact that he looks upon us, ex-prisoners, as lepers. He fills in on my Displaced Person's card "TB and VD negative"; this opens the first gate to the way home. The second one is called "screening".

A pale, blond captain in battledress only allows me to sit down when I indicate that standing is difficult for me. He asks and keeps on asking and rips off the membrane over my memory, which spews out all over him.

My DP (Displaced Person) card gets full. A letter giving me the right to obtain a travel document from the consulate without paying a fee and an address for clothes from the Dutch Mission comprise the morning's last exploits.

I arrive at the place at which I'm staying almost too late for mealtime. I don't have any ration coupons and am "advanced" a meal mistrustfully. The unwilling credit of guardians. I feel like Oliver Twist.

A vaguely familiar face from the past, deeply furrowed, with lively eyes, across the table from me. His name comes to me: Merksamer, one of the baggage handlers from Westerbork. Our mutual recognition is short and clear. Few sentences are needed to tell our stories. We only have to fill in the blanks. My hunger rumbles on after the meal. His too, but he knows what to do. He drags me with him to the Métro Victor Hugo. My first ride in the bowels of Paris is strangely familiar. When we get off at Jean Jaurès, he knows the way to a dilapidated building where food awaits us.

A plain room with tables and chairs. We're late. A big man in a caftan welcomes us and brings us to the soup, which seems to be in endless supply. We spoon it up greedily and tear off chunks of bread. Laughing paternally, he looks down at us. His Yiddish is an old fur, warm and comfortable. Friends swarm around us: "Where do you come from? Which camp? Did you see . . . from Lodz? . . . from Kielce? . . . from Bialystock?" Questions are swirling all around us; how little we have to tell. They urge us: stay here, you won't find anything back there. I'm made painfully aware of how much more they know than I, how widespread the slaughter was, how little there is left to search for.

We leave, satiated and at peace. An old man with a red beard and earlocks is standing at the entrance. He pushes twenty francs into my hand: "Take this, little friend, and buy something nice."

Back in the Dutch Reception Center, I stand in line for ration coupons. Thirty francs, our pocket money, is accompanied by advice to be frugal.

A feeling of wealth and freedom gives me the courage to refuse a pair of old army boots that are handed to me the next day at the Dutch Mission. What use are shoes that won't fit my bandaged foot? I accept a synthetic, loosely woven herringbone suit and some underwear. The suit is too small, but there's nothing else. I roam the city by métro and bus and sit on park benches in the sun, next to tramps and mothers spoiling their children.

I walk at a slow shuffle through the wide and inviting

streets, let hurried and curious people pass me by and know that the world is meant to be like this. I stand in front of display windows and stare my eyes out at the unobtainable. Shoe stores are magnets; how wonderful it would be . . . "Shoes" mean survival, freedom. What's money without shoes?

Not far from the Père Lachaise cemetery, I overcome my timorousness and step uncertainly into a shoe store. Two salesgirls look at me with laughter and gravity in their faces. My grubby head of stubble, shabby clothes and wooden clogs brand me as a beggar. Pointing and stuttering, I try to explain what I want. They fetch their boss, an older man, who explains to me in laborious French-German that leather shoes with leather soles can only be purchased with very special priority coupons. I persevere, show him my foot and lay bare a piece of my past. He casts aside his formality. Shoes with flexible wooden soles but with pliable leather uppers are rationed, but he's willing to overlook that.

The girls fetch box after box and try the shoes with infinite, friendly patience until they find some that fit me. I decide on a soft, chestnut-colored pair that smells heavenly. It would be a sin to christen them now; that has to happen slowly, festively. Giggling, they wrap up my costly treasure and wave to me from the door of the store until I disappear from view.

Overcome by a fierce longing, I open the paper while I'm walking. I want to touch the leather, inhale its aroma, admire and feel my treasure. My hand glides into a shoe and feels something strange, something that doesn't belong there. One package falls out and then another: Chesterfields. I now understand that their laughter betokened warmth, not derision, and I'm choked by tears of joy.

Paris is dazzling in July 1945. Bastille Day, 14 July, is a carousel of dancing soldiers and laughing girls in clean, freshly pressed blouses, of French waltzes played on the accordion and satisfied old people, of tramps and wounded war veterans. There is a bonfire at the Étoile and lanterns along the streets radiating from it. And everybody is happy.

I missed the parade, or perhaps I wanted to? My budding joy doesn't lend itself to soldiers' boots and marching music. It's also my day of liberation.

That evening, I hear that a train will be leaving for the Netherlands in a few days, a journey into the unknown that both attracts and frightens me.

I roam through Paris for one last embrace, treat myself to ice-cream at a sidewalk café and imagine myself to be a tourist. Near the Seine in the Latin Quarter, an old woman with a shawl and a long peasant dress is pushing a flat cart heaped with apricots, ripe and rosy yellow. She stands still, her customers like bees around the hive. For each one, she weighs the fruit on the scales, fashions a long cone out of a newspaper and rolls the apricots into it. I count the last of my money. Half a kilo, that ought to be enough, although the price per kilo appears to be steep. Since I don't know the French for half a kilo, I try to make my wish clear with gestures. She grins at me and fills the scale to bursting. I make a desperate attempt to explain it again: half a kilo and absolutely no more than that. But she continues, doesn't pay any attention to my gestures. She lays the great big paper cone full of fruit into my arms like a baby, and when I start to pay her, she refuses, laughing out loud, and wishes me "*bonne chance*".

The Brussels train is ready and waiting at the Gare du Nord. The dusty gray-green coaches are already nearly full, though most of the compartment doors are still open. I climb on the long running board, looking for an empty place. I walk from car to car, look in one compartment after another and hope that somebody will move over.

A Red Cross nurse helps me look, and near the end of the train, way beyond the dark roof of the station, I hear my name. In the tumult, I can't find where the voice is coming from. Then a nearby door is thrown open and I'm welcomed with a shout by André, Hans and two other friends from Prague. They persuade someone to make room, and I sit on the smooth wooden bench, deeply satisfied. The train moves off, panting and puffing, a long time after its official time of departure. We don't look up from the travel stories we're telling each other, for there's no one there to wave us goodbye.

The train chugs monotonously through Northern France. Sometimes fast, sometimes at a crawl. It frequently comes to a halt at a dilapidated station or in an immense wheat field. It's not quite dark when the suburbs of Brussels glide past the windows.

Documents in our hands, we wander slowly through the streets, looking for the place where we are to stay. A guide or helper shows the way, and near the hotel we see a street sign: rue Rauter. We swear loudly at the name of Holland and Belgium's highest-ranking SS officer.

We continue our journey the next day. It's cold and damp and the faces in the stations are overcast. No warmth flows toward us from the platforms. In the compartments, our ties begin to crumble, since our thoughts are elsewhere. In

Eindhoven, we're not passengers, but goods. We get out at a freight-car siding, next to a mammoth concrete building with small windows. A tall and menacing barbed-wire fence conjures up dark images.

A numbered, green label is hung around my neck.

We stand in long lines outside the train and, on command, walk to the entrance of a warehouse. A chilly camp atmosphere hangs there like a leaden cloud. Endless rooms without beds, without chairs. Dark straw mattresses on the stone floor, several yards long and several yards wide, like concrete flower beds. People in rumpled, musty clothes shuffle past. Some are sitting or lying down, never losing sight of their meager possessions. They tear off hunks of bread, write letters or read avidly so as not to hear the hum of voices. An occasional person sleeps as if nothing can disturb him, while another moans and grinds his teeth. Loudspeakers mounted on the ceilings blare out messages and call the names of those who must report at the counter. Sirens wail to indicate meals. People are lined up for the water faucets and toilets. A woman is weeping; she has been hoping for weeks for a message from "outside."

We all wait days or weeks like lost and found objects awaiting their owners. The office is in a room further away. Young men in uniforms or civilian clothes ask people questions, make lists and take notes. Sometimes someone disappears behind a locked door and doesn't come back. A wolf among the sheep, unmasked.

Small groups of people with bundles, on the point of departure. I watch them dejectedly and wait for my miracle: Where should I go? Who will come to claim me?

After several days, I hear my name from on high and jump like a guilty person. Behind the counter is a young man with a vaguely familiar face. His glance betrays recognition, shock, bashfulness. "Hey, it's Gerhard! Don't you remember me anymore? I'm Kuyt's son. Your father bought cigars from us, in Apeldoorn, on the Schuttersweg. I saw your name on the list."

The three years between then and now seem to be three hundred.

I shake his hand; a bit of home.

"Some people have turned up," he says cautiously, "but very few have come back from over there where you were, as far as I know. An uncle of yours and some cousins have surfaced!" He doesn't know where they are staying. He advises me to start looking in Apeldoorn and puts my name on the list for transport headed toward the northern part of the Netherlands.

The sun is above our heads. The steel hood of the US army truck is almost too hot to touch. The bed is so high that no one can climb up without help. Once aboard we sit like migrants on our bundles, with handkerchiefs as sun bonnets. Rumbling, trailing dust and stones. The mammoth ten-ton truck drives me and many others like me to the places that we were hounded out of long, long ago. They get out all along the route: Nijmegen, Arnhem, Deventer, Zwolle. Each time, the parting is swift. A waving hand, a goodbye, best wishes. We're extremely adept at saying farewell.

The last part is long and lonely. I'm the only passenger, sitting very small and still in the cabin next to the soldier. He remains tactfully silent when we reach Apeldoorn. From my high position, I see the lanes and the paths, the old white houses and my school, the grocery where as a boy I bought things for my mother and the place where I read a fragment from the Book of Judges and received the rights accorded Jewish males.

The truck comes to a halt in Market Square, across from the brick building with barred windows and round gates: the police station.

Three years ago the beginning, and now the end, of a journey.

EPILOGUE

There are few eyewitness reports that go beyond liberation or capitulation.

Only rarely did anyone speak of homecoming, except for Jews from Poland or Russia, since for many of them "homecoming" was synonymous with insult and expulsion, murder and death.

For three hundred and fifty of the Jews who had survived the Nazi war crimes, the year of liberation ended in violent death in their native countries. The only pogroms to make the foreign press[23] were in Cracow and Kielce. Poland was a fertile ground for fanatical anti-Semites and greedy non-Jews to whom possessions had been entrusted for safekeeping. The authorities either stood by helplessly or turned a blind eye to their refusal to return these possessions and to the bloody pogroms.

The fact that only a few stripes appeared in the sky above Auschwitz in September of 1944 can be attributed to the same political impotence, the same national autism. After the war as well as during it, the Jews were left to their fate at home and abroad.

Our reports usually ended at an earlier period, because everything that happened to us after May 1945 could only be good and beautiful compared to previous events. Doubts as to whether our homecoming had really been so wonderful only arose years afterwards.

In 1945, the speed with which liberated Jewish prisoners were helped to return varied from country to country, as did the enthusiasm with which they were greeted. On the thermometer scale of humanity, the Netherlands assumed a place somewhere in the middle. The East bloc countries were located way below the freezing point. Only the Scandinavian countries immediately made every effort on behalf of their deported citizens and even many of the stateless.

While private individuals, such as Frank Hanepen[24] and Dr Polak Daniëls,[25] though lacking any official status, accomplished the nearly impossible task in Czechoslovakia in 1945 of organizing the repatriation of their Dutch compatriots, a Repatriation Commission was set up by the Dutch government only in October of that year.

When we arrived home, we turned out to be travelers with an impoverished vocabulary. We lacked the language to describe our experiences. The worn-out words that did exist did not get uttered, for virtually nobody was there to hear them and virtually nobody wanted to listen to them, let alone try to comprehend them. They would spoil the glow of liberation and expose the self-deceit of many.

It was not until seventeen years after his liberation that

Primo Levi, looking back on a year of imprisonment in Auschwitz and a nine-month odyssey through the chaotic Europe of 1945, described his homecoming: "I reached Turin on 19 October, after thirty-five days of travel; my house was still standing, all my family was alive, no one was expecting me. I was swollen, bearded and in rags, and had difficulty in making myself recognized. I found my friends full of life, the warmth of secure meals, the solidity of daily work, the liberating joy of recounting my story."[26]

I read his account with amazement and a feeling of self-pity. How different, how bleak the end of my journey was.

My house was still standing. The occupants, recipients in 1943 of privileges from the occupying forces, did not allow me to cross the threshold. My parents and the other residents of our house were "missing." My aunt, rescued from Ravensbrück by Folke Bernadotte with the Swedish Red Cross, was sick in Malmö. A few family members who no longer expected me turned up. Highly principled friends of my parents and neighbors, some decent and some not, each had their own story of the hardships of the occupation which made me choke back the unspeakable. I was the near stranger who had to listen to everything that everyone else had heard over and over again, and I bought acceptance with my willing ear and discreet silence.

I learned to live like a human being among people again, found hospitality, sometimes even warmth, and bricked up the past in my memory. Why, after nearly forty years, the mortar is no longer holding is a question I leave to others. The shocking memories which I, thanks to understanding therapists, can once again allow in my thoughts and emotions need to be corroborated by those of my former fellow prisoners, through oral and written reports.

I wanted—and still want—to know the why and wherefore of our catastrophe and to use these to get to know my own coordinates. How did we live and survive, what was our liberation like, what kind of homecoming did we have? And why was the world blind and deaf in the darkest hours of the war and after?

Research in libraries and archives left many questions unanswered, and many of the answers caused great pain.

NOTES

1 Block Head. A prisoner (usually a criminal or political prisoner) assigned to head a block or barrack.

2 Block Leader. A noncommissioned SS officer charged with counting prisoners, assisting during selections and punishments, etc.

3 Special units. SS troops under the command of Jost and Blum. These killing squads followed the army into Poland, the Baltic states and in 1941 into Russia, murdering 2.5 million Jews.

4 Book purportedly written by Herman Rauschning, one of the first top-ranking Nazis (later an adversary), in which Hitler discusses his plans for Europe and the Jews.

5 Military Police. Their duties included arresting and guarding Jews and political prisoners, taking hostages and carrying out executions.

6 On 1 January 1939 a Nazi law assigned all German and stateless male Jews the middle name "Israël" and females the name "Sarah."

7 Western Holland's line of defense, based on flood control. To check an enemy invasion, the land lying within the line of fortifications could be inundated. However, the German air attacks made the system superfluous.

8 Prof Dr David Cohen. Chairman of the Dutch Jewish Council from 1941 to 1943 and a "prominent" prisoner and member of the Council of Elders in Theresienstadt. After the war, the Jewish Honorary Council denied him the right to hold Jewish offices on the grounds of his dubious attitude towards the occupying forces.

9 Camp Kapo. Prisoner of general service to the *Lagerälteste*, who was likewise a prisoner, directly responsible to the SS for the internal organization of the camp compound.

10 Confinement to barracks. Every prisoner was required to go to his or her block or barrack and to stay inside until the sirens wailed.

11 Johan Schwarzhuber. The SS commandant of Auschwitz II-Birkenau.

12 Josef Mengele. The SS Chief Medical Officer. His role in the selections and his numerous medical experiments on twins and adults have made his name notorious.

13 "Muslims." A term frequently used among prisoners to refer to the weak and inept likely to fall prey to selection.

14 Fritz Buntrock. An SS *Scharführer* and Birkenau's *Rapportführer* (Reporting Officer).

15 Barrack personnel. Prisoners (assigned by the *Blockälteste*) in charge of distributing the food and keeping the barracks clean.

16 The prisoners were divided into various color-coded categories and were required to wear corresponding triangular cloth badges sewn on to their jackets and trousers. Color key: red = political prisoners, green = common criminals, yellow = Jews, pink = homosexuals, black = Gypsies or other so-called antisocial elements. Camp inmates commonly referred to people as "red triangles," "green triangles," etc.

17 RSHA (*Reichs Sicherheits Hauptamt*). Head office for Reich Security. First the headquarters of Reinhardt Heydrich and later of Heinrich Himmler.

18 Joachim von Ribbentrop. Minister of Foreign Affairs under Hitler.

19 See Footnote 5.

20 Together with the Gestapo, the *Sicherheitspolizei* constituted the Security Police, while the SD or *Sicherheitsdienst* (Security Service) formed the Political Department of the SS.

21 Research conducted into the IRC archives in Geneva in 1988 revealed that Dr Rossel was a staunch Nazi sympathizer.

22 Under Minister Fritz Todt and his successor Albert Speer, this paramilitary organization constructed the German autobahn system and the concentration camps.

23 For extensive documentation, see: *European Jewry Ten Years After the War*, New York 1956; Lucjan Dobroszycki, "Restoring Jewish Life in Postwar Poland", in *Soviet Jewish Affairs*, Vol. 3, No. 2, 1973; Bernard D. Weinryb, "Poland", in *The Jews in the Soviet Satellites*, Syracuse 1953.

24 Frank Hanepen was forty-seven years old in 1945 and already had a long career in journalism behind him. As Foreign Correspondent for *De Telegraaf* in London until 1933 and for the *News Chronicle* and the *New York Times* in Vienna until September 1938, he foretold much of Europe's catastrophic history. Several months after Hitler's annexation of Austria, Hanepen left for Prague. Until 10 May 1940, he wrote articles for the *New York Times* and United Press that eventually landed him in the Gestapo prison in Prague.

After his release in February 1941, he remained free until October 1942, but was once again arrested on the grounds of "illegal" activities, which included help to Jews.

He had to abandon his journalism from July 1943 until May 1945.

Thousands of former concentration camp inmates, forced laborers and DPs, sick, wounded and hungry, without papers and without money, waited that summer in Prague for care and transport home. This included more than a thousand Dutch citizens who had to make do without any diplomatic representation or repatriation service. For months, Frank Hanepen tirelessly and imperturbably arranged food, accommodation, medical care, emergency papers, and above all, transport to the West.

His rescue activities were helped by the fact that he was on friendly terms with the Secretary of the Interior, with whom he had been imprisoned in the Gestapo prison, and with many loyal Czechs. When the first post-war representative, Merens, took up office in the fall of 1945 and the official Repatriation Commission was set up in October 1945, he continued his work, now legalized.

In 1947, his sacrifices received well-deserved recognition: Frank Hanepen was awarded a Knighthood in the Order of Oranje Nassau.

He died poor and disillusioned in 1973. The Netherlands had forgotten him, just as it had forgotten its subjects in Prague in the spring and summer of 1945.

25 In the fall of 1942, the half-Jewish doctor, Dr A. Polak Daniëls, was called to attend to a patient who could not cope with the message that her daughter had been sent from Westerbork to Auschwitz. This direct confrontation with the Final Solution to the Jewish Question affected the relatively safe doctor (whose parents had taken their own lives in May 1940) so deeply that he decided to form medical aid teams to care for the prisoners after liberation. As Assistant Director of the Red Cross Hospital, he managed to convince the Director, Dr H.K. Offerhaus, of the necessity of such teams. The plans for a relief team from Switzerland were formulated in a letter addressed to the Dutch delegate in Bern, J.J.B. Bosch Ridder van Rosenthal.

The war lasted longer than Polak Daniëls could have suspected. At the end of 1943, he and his future wife escaped to Switzerland with the help of French and Dutch resistance groups in order to direct the recruitment and training of the medical aid teams. To his dismay, he discovered upon his arrival that no action had been taken to his letter. Backed by M.H. Gans and Dr Visser 't Hooft, but without the actual support of the Dutch government in London and its representative, Polak Daniëls set up his aid team. These volunteers were given no chance to carry out the important task that they had set for themselves.

Specious arguments and personal and political interests scuttled the well-intentioned plan, which could have saved so many lives. Disillusioned, but not discouraged, Polak Daniëls remained in Switzerland until the German surrender. With the help of French friends, he flew to London, where he was granted the rank of major, and then to Prague.

By virtue of his inventiveness and dedication, his ability to improvise and his good communication skills, he succeeded (working closely with Frank Hanepen, whom he had met immediately after his arrival in Prague) in procuring medical care and transport to the West for numerous ex-concentration camp prisoners.

26 Primo Levi, *The Truce*, Penguin Books, London 1979, page 379.

BIBLIOGRAPHY

H.G. Adler, *Theresienstadt 1941-1945: Das Antlitz einer Zwangsgemein-schaft*, 2nd printing, J.C.B. Mohr, Tübingen 1960.

H.G. Adler, *Die Verheimlichte Wahrheit*, Theresienstädter Dokumente, J.C.B. Mohr, Tübingen 1958.

J. Bacon, "Mit der Neugier von Kindern", in *Auschwitz, Zeugnisse und Berichte*, Europäische Verlaganstalt, Frankfurt/Main 1962.

Martin Gilbert, *Auschwitz and the Allies: How the Allies Responded to the News of Hitler's Final Solution*, Michael Joseph/Rainbird, London 1981 and Holt, Rinehart & Winston, New York 1981.

L. de Jong, *Het Koninkrijk der Nederlanden in de Tweede Wereldoorlog: Gevangenen en Gedeporteerden*, Vol. 8, 2nd half, Martinus Nijhoff, The Hague 1978.

O.D. Kulka, *Getuigenverslag Auschwitz Proces*, Frankfurt/Main 1964 (30.07.1964). Yad Vashem Archives, Jerusalem Nr. 03/2896.

O.D. Kulka, *Ghetto in an Annihilation Camp*, mimeo Yad Vashem, Jerusalem 1980.

H. Langbein, *Der Auschwitzprozess: Eine Dokumentation*, Europa Verlag, Vienna 1965.

H. Langbein, *Menschen in Auschwitz*, Europa Verlag, Vienna 1972.

Walter Laqueur, *The Terrible Secret: An Investigation into the Suppression of Information About Hitler's "Final Solution"*, Weidenfeld & Nicolson, London 1980.

Z. Lederer, *Ghetto Theresienstadt*, E. Goldson & Son Ltd., London 1953.

Heiner Lichtenstein, *Warum Auschwitz nicht bombardiert wurde (Mit einem Vorwort von Eugen Kogon)*, Bund Verlag, Cologne 1980.

R. Oppenheym, *Theresienstädter Tagebuch: An der Grenze des Lebens*, Rütten & Loening Verlag, Hamburg 1961.

J. Presser, *The Destruction of the Dutch Jews*, Dutton, New York 1965.

G. Reitlinger, *Die Endlösung*, Colloquium Verlag, Berlin 1979.

W. Rings, *Leben mit dem Feind: Anpassung und Widerstand in Hitlers Europa*, Kindler Verlag, Munich 1979.

Bernard Wasserstein, *Britain and the Jews of Europe 1939–1945*, Clarendon Press, Oxford 1979.

David S. Wyman, "Why Auschwitz Was Never Bombed", in *Commentary*, May 1978.

"Letters from Readers: Bombing Auschwitz", in *Commentary*, July 1978.